THE
OCEANS
ATLAS

By Anita Ganeri
Illustrated by Luciano Corbella

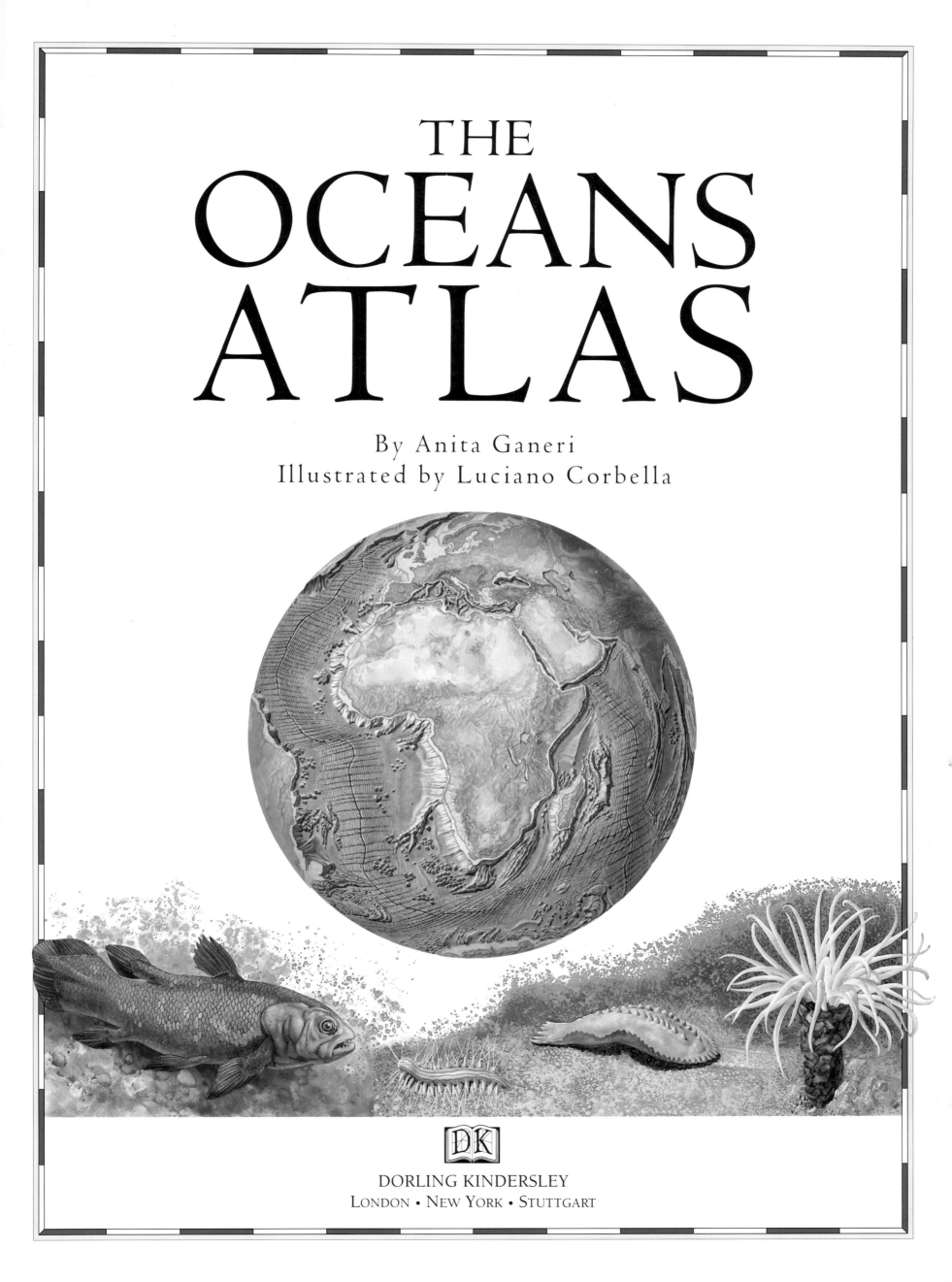

DK

DORLING KINDERSLEY
LONDON · NEW YORK · STUTTGART

A DORLING KINDERSLEY BOOK

Art Editor Rachael Foster
Project Editors John C. Miles and Laura Buller
US Editor B. Alison Weir
Production Shelagh Gibson
Managing Editor Susan Peach
Managing Art Editor Jacquie Gulliver
Oceanographic Consultant Brian Bett

First American Edition, 1994
2 6 8 10 9 7 5

Published in the United States by Dorling Kindersley, Inc.
232 Madison Avenue, New York, New York 10016

Library of Congress Cataloging-in-Publication Data

Ganeri, Anita, 1961–
The oceans atlas / written by Anita Ganeri;
illustrated by Luciano Corbella. —
1st American ed.
p. cm.
Includes index.
ISBN 1-56458-475-5
1. Ocean—Juvenile literature. [1. Ocean.]
I. Corbella, Luciano, ill. II. Title.
GC21.5. G35 1994
551.46—dc20   93-28724
CIP
AC

Reproduced in Hong Kong
by Bright Arts

Printed and bound in Italy
by New Interlitho, Milan

Contents

Earth or Ocean?

IF YOU COULD JOURNEY into space and look back homeward, you might think that "Ocean" would be a more accurate name for our planet than "Earth." Over two-thirds of its surface is covered in seawater, making it the most watery planet in the solar system. The water lies in five oceans. In order of size, they are the Pacific, Atlantic, Indian, Antarctic, and Arctic. They form a continuous expanse of sea, broken up by the continents.

The tallest mountain, the deepest trench, and the longest mountain range on Earth are all found in its oceans. With this book, you can explore the oceans from shore to seafloor, and find out about the amazing landscapes and creatures under the waves.

This picture looks blue because the blue portion of light penetrates the farthest distance under water.

LETTING IN LIGHT

When sunlight hits the sea, some of the rays are reflected back up into the sky. The rest are absorbed by the water. Tiny particles in the water scatter the various colors in the light. The diagram below shows how colors are absorbed. Red is absorbed first, so it only reaches a short distance into the water. Blue is the last to be absorbed, so it reaches farthest. Even in clear water, however, very little sunlight can reach below 820 ft (250 m).

Red | Orange | Yellow | Green | Blue | Indigo

North Sea

The North Sea is the site of many undersea oil and gas fields. The extraction of this oil and gas has been a major challenge to technology because of the depths and the treacherous seas involved.

North Atlantic Ocean

The North Atlantic has been a major shipping route between Europe and North America for centuries. It is also one of the world's main fishing grounds.

Sargasso Sea

The Sargasso Sea is a sea within a sea in a calm, warm area of the mid-Atlantic. In places it is covered with sargassum weed, a plant that floats in clumps on the surface with the help of small, air-filled bladders that look like grapes.

Atlantis

Some people believe that a fabulous, ancient city called Atlantis once existed in the middle of the Atlantic Ocean. The city was supposed to have been destroyed by a massive earthquake, and slipped beneath the waves without a trace.

GREENLAND ARCTIC OCEAN

NORTH SEA

BALTIC SEA

EUROPE

Bay of Biscay

NORTH ATLANTIC OCEAN

Strait of Gibraltar

MEDITERRANEAN SEA

BLACK SEA

CASPIAN SEA

ARAL SEA

ASIA

Canary Islands

SARGASSO SEA

Cape Verde Islands

AFRICA

RED SEA

ARABIA

PERSIAN GULF

ARABIAN SEA

BAY OF BENGAL

INDIAN OCEAN

GULF OF GUINEA

SOUTH AMERICA

SOUTH ATLANTIC OCEAN

MOZAMBIQUE CHANNEL

MADAGASCAR

SCOTIA SEA

ANTARCTIC OCEAN

WEDDELL SEA

ANTARCTICA

Persian Gulf

This entire area was hit by severe oil pollution following the Gulf War, in 1991. Seabirds and marine life in particular were badly affected.

Colorful seas

Not all seas appear to be blue. The Black Sea, on the borders of Europe and Asia, looks black because the mud it contains is rich in hydrogen sulfide. The Red Sea gets its name from the red plants that sometimes bloom on its surface.

Antarctic Ocean

The Antarctic Ocean surrounds the continent of Antarctica. It is home to many of the world's great whales, now in danger of extinction, and hundreds of thousands of seabirds, such as albatrosses and penguins. It is freezing cold and whipped by high winds in the winter, producing mountainous seas.

SEAWATER DENSITY

Density measures how heavy something is for its size. The gas form of most substances is less dense than the liquid form, which is less dense than the solid form. If you put all three in a beaker, the gas would float on the liquid, which would float on the solid (see top beaker). But water is different. Its liquid form is denser than its solid form, ice. The solid ice floats on the liquid water, topped by the gas form, water vapor (see bottom beaker).

Gas

Liquid

Solid

Water vapor

Ice

Water

SALTWATER SOUP

The salty taste of seawater is due to the large amounts of sodium chloride, or common salt, dissolved in it. But seawater also contains smaller quantities of other "salts," including sulfate, magnesium, calcium, and potassium. The saltiness, or salinity, of seawater is measured as the number of grams of salts in 2.2 lb (1 kg) of water. This is written as ‰. The average salinity of the oceans is about 35 ‰.

2.2 lb (1 kg) of seawater

Other — Bicarbonate — Potassium — Calcium
Magnesium — Sulfate
Sodium
Chloride

Salts in 2.2 lb (1 kg) of seawater

Bering Strait

The narrow Bering Strait connects the Arctic Ocean with the north Pacific Ocean. Millions of years ago, Asia and North America were joined by a bridge of land here. Today, the land is submerged beneath the strait.

Great gulfs

A gulf is part of an ocean that "dents" the land, whether in a gentle curve such as the Gulf of Alaska, or a narrow arm such as the Gulf of California.

Volcanic islands

The Pacific Ocean floor is marked with chains of underwater volcanoes that break the surface to form island groups. There are thousands of these islands. Some, such as the Hawaiian Islands, are home to large numbers of people, while others are almost uninhabited.

Island eruptions

Violent volcanic eruptions are sometimes felt on the islands of the Caribbean Sea. In 1902, Mt. Pelée exploded with a shower of glowing hot gas, devastating the city of St. Pierre, Martinique, and killing all but two of its 29,000 residents.

Pacific Ocean

Covering an area twice the size of the Atlantic, the Pacific Ocean is the largest ocean by far. It covers about one-third of the globe. At its widest point, the Pacific reaches nearly halfway around the world.

Galápagos Islands

The Galápagos are one of the few island groups in the eastern Pacific Ocean. The six main islands in this group are inhabited by unique wildlife that has evolved in isolation, including giant tortoises and exotic marine lizards.

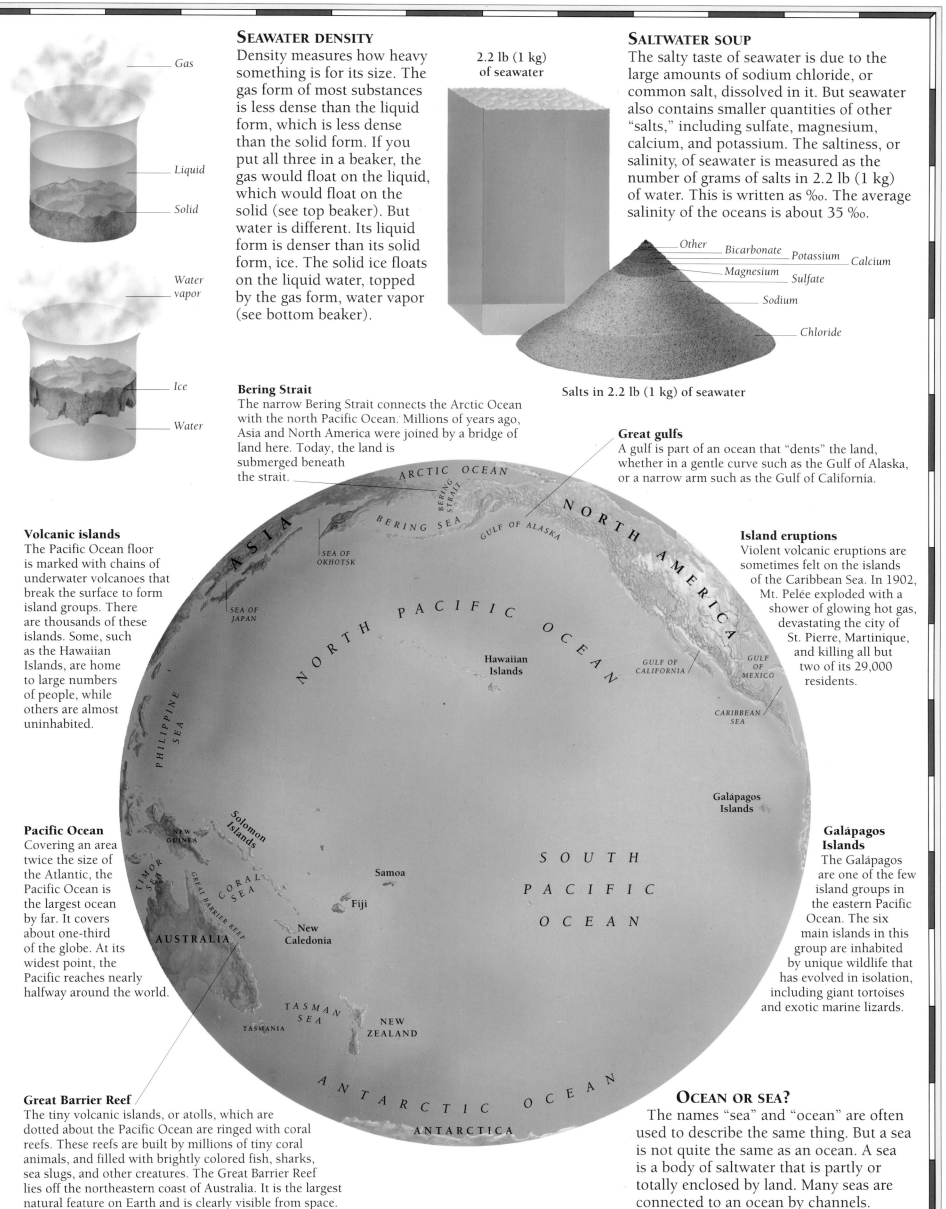

Great Barrier Reef

The tiny volcanic islands, or atolls, which are dotted about the Pacific Ocean are ringed with coral reefs. These reefs are built by millions of tiny coral animals, and filled with brightly colored fish, sharks, sea slugs, and other creatures. The Great Barrier Reef lies off the northeastern coast of Australia. It is the largest natural feature on Earth and is clearly visible from space.

OCEAN OR SEA?

The names "sea" and "ocean" are often used to describe the same thing. But a sea is not quite the same as an ocean. A sea is a body of saltwater that is partly or totally enclosed by land. Many seas are connected to an ocean by channels.

Earth Exposed

WITH ALL OF ITS WATER REMOVED, the Earth looks strange and barren. On the maps below, the enormous basins that the oceans normally fill are shown empty, exposing huge, mountainous ridges that snake across the surface, as well as great gashes, called trenches, that cut deep into the Earth's crust. In addition to these features there are giant underwater volcanoes, vast, barren areas known as abyssal plains, and flat-topped sea plateaus. All these features are the result of movements of the seafloor, including earthquakes and volcanic activity in the Earth's crust, which change the shape of the ocean basins over hundreds of thousands of years.

UNDER PRESSURE

The deeper you go underwater, the greater the weight of the water pressing on you. Air puts pressure on too. At sea level, air pressure is equivalent to 14.7 pounds pressing down on each square inch (or a 1 kg weight per each square centimeter). This measurement is known as one atmosphere.

Underwater, pressure increases by one atmosphere for every 33 ft (10 m) you descend. At 9,842 ft (3,000 m) the pressure is about 300 times as great as at sea level. Divers can only descend this far if they are protected inside thick-walled submarines or other underwater craft. Otherwise the pressure would crush them.

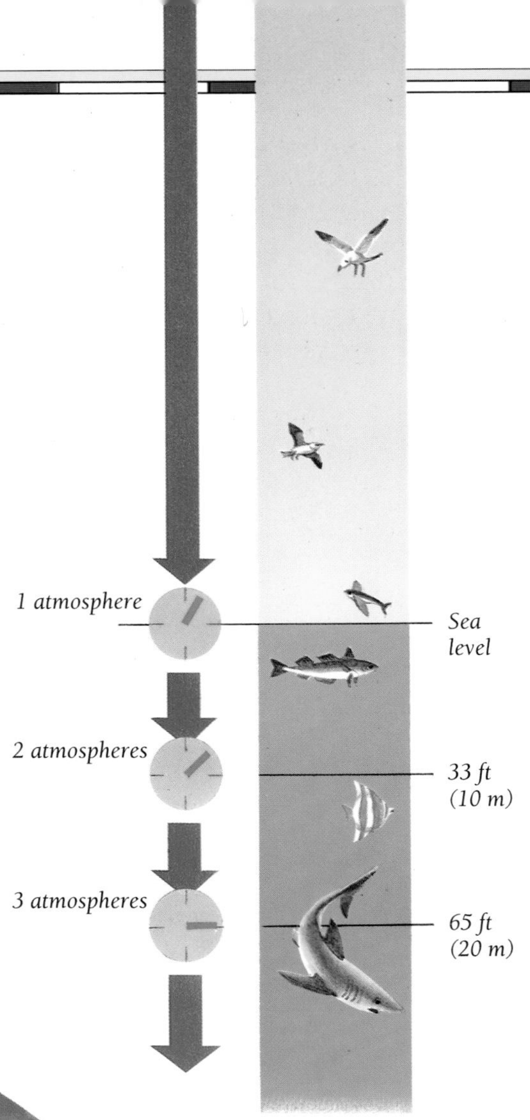

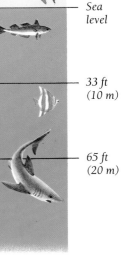

1 atmosphere — Sea level

2 atmospheres — 33 ft (10 m)

3 atmospheres — 65 ft (20 m)

Continental shelves
Both Europe and the east coast of North America are surrounded by projecting shelves of land, called continental shelves. The sea is quite shallow in these areas.

Mediterranean Basin
About seven million years ago, the Mediterranean was cut off from the Atlantic Ocean and dried up. The age of its seabed rocks indicates that the sea has actually flooded and dried up again many times.

Amazon Fan
Fans occur where a large river deposits sediment in the sea at the edge of a continent.

Mid-Atlantic Ridge
The surface of the Earth is made up of vast plates of rock. Mid-ocean ridges mark the places where two of these plates meet underwater. The Mid-Atlantic Ridge is the longest mountain chain in the world.

Basins
A huge, bowl-shaped dent in the ocean floor is called a basin.

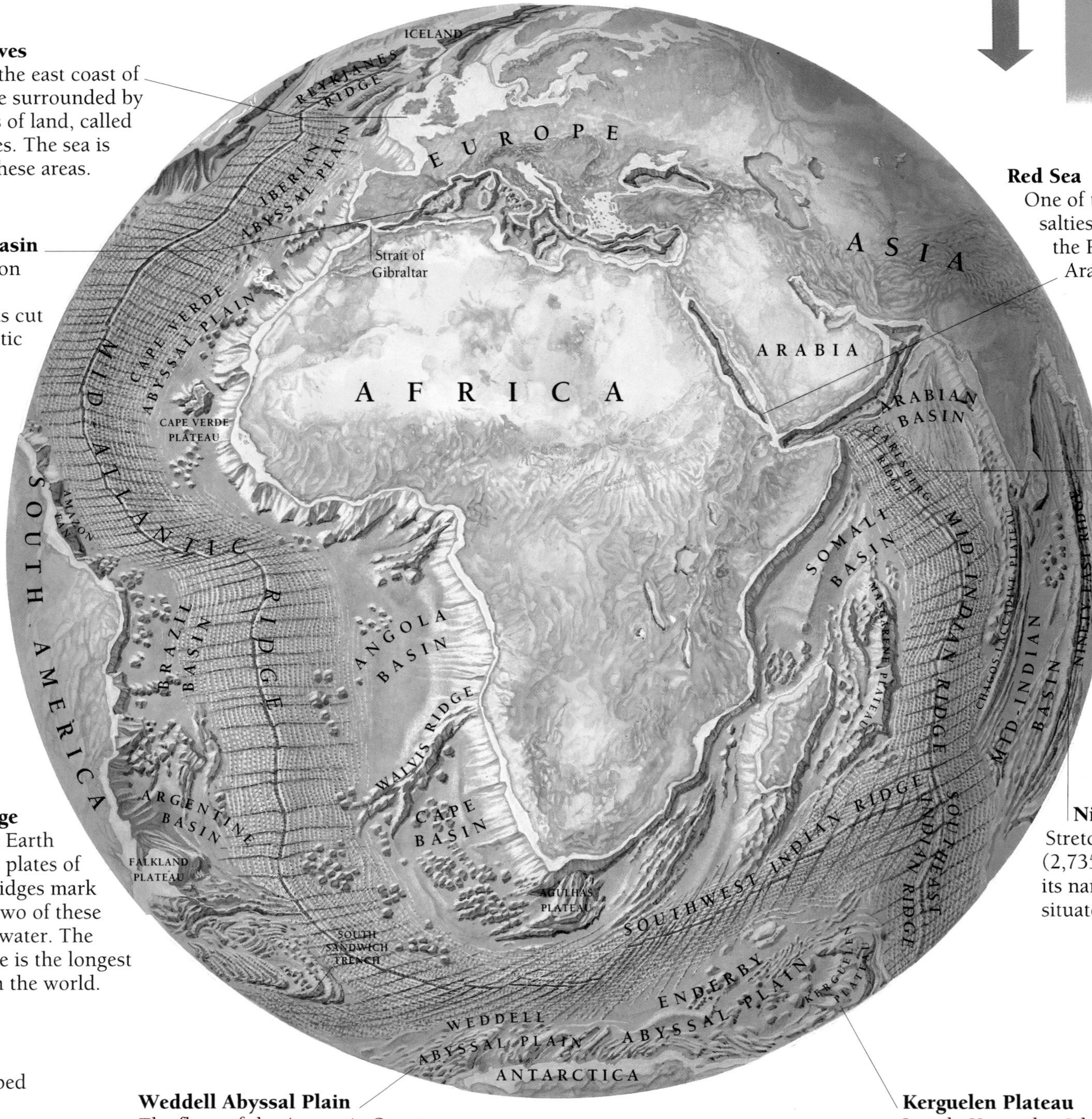

Red Sea
One of the youngest and saltiest of the world's seas, the Red Sea, formed when Arabia split from Africa.

Carlsberg Ridge
This ridge is the northernmost part of the Indian Ocean ridge system, which forms a huge, inverted "Y" shape.

Ninety East Ridge
Stretching over 1,700 miles (2,735 km), this ridge gets its name because it is situated on longitude 90°E.

Weddell Abyssal Plain
The floor of the Antarctic Ocean, surrounding Antarctica, is mainly vast, featureless abyssal plains. These are flat or very gently sloping areas found on the ocean floor.

Kerguelen Plateau
Lonely Kerguelen Island sits on this plateau. Once a center of the whaling industry, it is now a home for seabirds and other wildlife.

Map labels: ICELAND, REYKJANES RIDGE, EUROPE, ASIA, IBERIAN ABYSSAL PLAIN, Strait of Gibraltar, ARABIA, AFRICA, CAPE VERDE ABYSSAL PLAIN, CAPE VERDE PLATEAU, ARABIAN BASIN, MID-ATLANTIC RIDGE, SOUTH AMERICA, ANGOLA BASIN, SOMALI BASIN, BRAZIL BASIN, CARLSBERG RIDGE, WALVIS RIDGE, MID-INDIAN RIDGE, MID-INDIAN BASIN, NINETY EAST RIDGE, ARGENTINE BASIN, CAPE BASIN, FALKLAND PLATEAU, AGULHAS PLATEAU, SOUTHWEST INDIAN RIDGE, SOUTHEAST INDIAN RIDGE, SOUTH SANDWICH TRENCH, ENDERBY ABYSSAL PLAIN, WEDDELL ABYSSAL PLAIN, ANTARCTICA

UPS AND DOWNS

This chart shows relative high and low points on our planet, from the deepest depth in the Mariana Trench, to the highest height, Mount Everest. The average height of the Earth's surface, including that which is usually submerged beneath the oceans, comes out below sea level, showing just how deep the oceans really are.

Deepest depth Mariana Trench 35,827 ft (10,920 m)

Average ocean depth 12,237 ft (3,730 m)

Average height of Earth's surface 7,873 ft (2,400 m) below sea level

Average land height 2,854 ft (870 m)

Highest height Mount Everest 29,029 ft (8,848 m)

AMAZING OCEAN FACTS

❏ The Pacific Ocean holds more than half the seawater on Earth – almost as much as the Atlantic and Indian oceans combined.

❏ The Arctic Ocean is the smallest ocean. It is about 13 times smaller than the Pacific and contains just one percent of the Earth's seawater.

❏ About 97 percent of all the water on Earth is found in its oceans.

❏ Only 29 percent of the Earth is dry land. Together, Africa and Europe cover about 15,670,000 sq miles (40,600,000 sq km). Yet this is only half the size of the Atlantic, the second largest ocean.

❏ The length of the world's coastlines is about 312,000 miles (504,000 km), enough to circle the Equator 12 times.

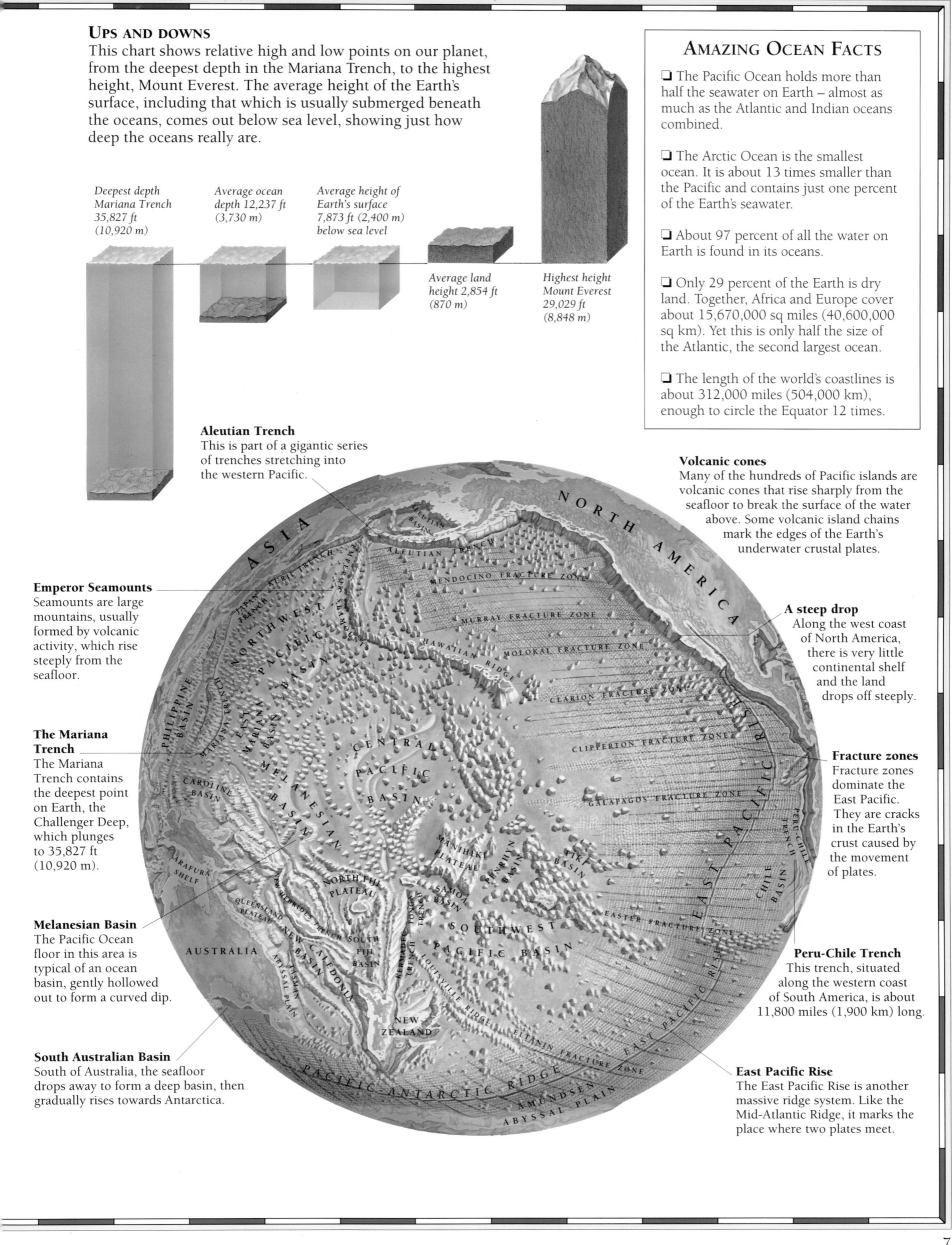

Aleutian Trench
This is part of a gigantic series of trenches stretching into the western Pacific.

Emperor Seamounts
Seamounts are large mountains, usually formed by volcanic activity, which rise steeply from the seafloor.

The Mariana Trench
The Mariana Trench contains the deepest point on Earth, the Challenger Deep, which plunges to 35,827 ft (10,920 m).

Melanesian Basin
The Pacific Ocean floor in this area is typical of an ocean basin, gently hollowed out to form a curved dip.

South Australian Basin
South of Australia, the seafloor drops away to form a deep basin, then gradually rises towards Antarctica.

Volcanic cones
Many of the hundreds of Pacific islands are volcanic cones that rise sharply from the seafloor to break the surface of the water above. Some volcanic island chains mark the edges of the Earth's underwater crustal plates.

A steep drop
Along the west coast of North America, there is very little continental shelf and the land drops off steeply.

Fracture zones
Fracture zones dominate the East Pacific. They are cracks in the Earth's crust caused by the movement of plates.

Peru-Chile Trench
This trench, situated along the western coast of South America, is about 11,800 miles (1,900 km) long.

East Pacific Rise
The East Pacific Rise is another massive ridge system. Like the Mid-Atlantic Ridge, it marks the place where two plates meet.

Moving Plates

THE EARTH'S HARD, OUTER LAYER, called the crust, is cracked into seven gigantic and many smaller pieces, called plates. In 1915, the German scientist Alfred Wegener put forward a theory that millions of years ago all the land on Earth was joined together as a single continent, Pangaea. It was surrounded by a huge ocean, called Panthalassa. As the plates of crust drifted apart, Pangaea split up, forming the oceans and continents we know today.

Until the 1960s, Wegener's theory was not taken seriously. Then scientists discovered that the plates do move on the semi-molten rocks below. They also found fossil evidence that supported the idea that the continents were once linked. As the plates drifted, they opened up the ocean basins. The size and shape of these basins are still changing today.

WHERE THE WATER CAME FROM

The Earth formed about 4,600 million years ago from a cloud of hot gases and dust. As the Earth cooled and solidified, water vapor was thrown into the atmosphere by volcanoes on its surface. The water vapor condensed to form storm clouds, and torrential rain filled the first oceans. This seawater was not cool and salty as it is today, but very hot and as acidic as vinegar.

Lithosphere

PACIFIC PLATE

Upper mantle
The rocks of the upper mantle are partly melted. They flow very slowly, like thick syrup.

Upper mantle (630 km) 390 miles

Lower mantle
Below about 90 miles (150 km), the rocks of the lower mantle are dense and solid.

Lower mantle 1,420 miles (2,290 km)

Outer core
The outer core is made up of molten iron and nickel. Scientists know it is liquid because of the way earthquake waves pass through it.

Outer core 1,130 miles (1,820 km)

Inner core
The center of the Earth is a solid ball of iron and nickel. Despite temperatures of up to 8,100°F (4,500°C), the inner core remains solid because of the immense pressure of the layers above it.

Inner core 995 miles (1,600 km)

THE EARTH'S LAYERS
The Earth is made up of several layers, which fit one around the other. These layers form three main sections: the crust, the mantle, and the core. The outermost layer is a brittle shell called the lithosphere. A cross-section of the lithosphere is shown below. It is made up of the crust and the molten rocks of the upper mantle. The upper mantle wraps around the lower mantle, which in turn surrounds the outer and inner cores (see left).

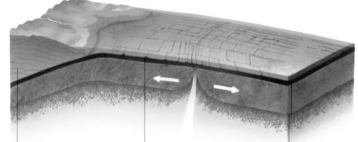

The crust under the continents is on average about 25 miles (40 km) thick. At its deepest it can reach a depth of 43 miles (70 km).

Crust under the oceans is only about 3 miles (5 km) thick.

Lithosphere

HOW THE PLATES MOVE
The plates of the crust drift on the mantle, driven by heat from deep inside the Earth. Everything on the Earth's surface – from the continents to the ocean basins – is carried along on the plates. This means that all the features on Earth are created as the plates pull apart from each other or collide. Mountains are pushed up by two plates crashing into each other. Earthquakes and volcanoes happen at the edges of plates. Where two plates pull apart, molten rock from the mantle wells up to plug the gap.

Surtsey, off southwest Iceland

The surface evidence
Although it is difficult to imagine continents and oceans being carried along on gigantic plates, there is some visible evidence of plate movement. The photograph of Thingvellir, Iceland (right), shows ravines and cliffs that mark the edges of two plates: the North American Plate and the Eurasian Plate. The two plates are slowly pulling apart, cutting a rift across Iceland and causing frequent volcanoes and earthquakes. This same plate movement was also responsible for the massive undersea volcano that formed the island of Surtsey.

Earth 200 million years ago
After hundreds of millions of years, the plates settled some 300 million years ago to form Pangaea and Panthalassa, the world ocean. Pangaea began to split up about 200 million years ago.

Earth 180 million years ago
Pangaea split into two landmasses separated by the Tethys Sea about 180 million years ago: Laurasia in the north, and Gondwanaland in the south. A Y-shaped rift began to divide Gondwanaland.

Earth 65 million years ago
Further plate movements opened the Atlantic, Indian, and Antarctic oceans. Panthalassa shrank to half its original size and became the Pacific Ocean, while the Tethys became the Mediterranean Sea.

SPREADING CONTINENTS
Between 65 million years ago and the present day, Greenland split from Europe, and Australia drifted from Antarctica. The map below shows the current position of the plates. The key describes what happens where two plates meet. At a spreading ridge, the plates move apart and new crust forms to fill the gap. At a subduction zone, the plates are forced together. Crust from one of the plates is carried down (subducted) into the mantle. At transform faults, no crust is made or destroyed. Instead, the plates grind past each other, creating deep cracks.

Earth 50 million years from now
What might tomorrow's world look like? The eastern part of Africa may split off along the line of its rift valley, while the rest of the continent moves northward and closes the Mediterranean. Australia could nudge closer to Asia, and a sliver of western North America might slide up the coast.

KEY TO PLATE BOUNDARIES
⊢⊢⊢⊢	SPREADING RIDGE
▲▲▲▲	SUBDUCTION ZONE
———	TRANSFORM FAULT
- - -	UNCERTAIN BOUNDARY
➤	MOVEMENT OF PLATE

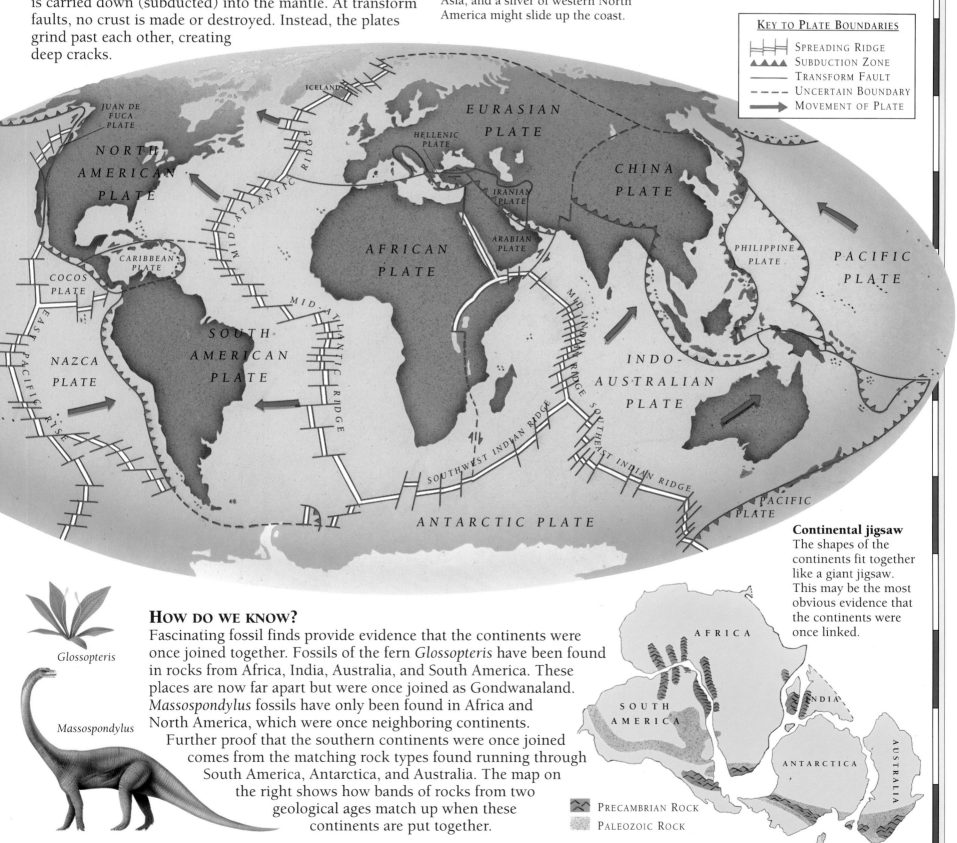

HOW DO WE KNOW?
Fascinating fossil finds provide evidence that the continents were once joined together. Fossils of the fern *Glossopteris* have been found in rocks from Africa, India, Australia, and South America. These places are now far apart but were once joined as Gondwanaland. *Massospondylus* fossils have only been found in Africa and North America, which were once neighboring continents. Further proof that the southern continents were once joined comes from the matching rock types found running through South America, Antarctica, and Australia. The map on the right shows how bands of rocks from two geological ages match up when these continents are put together.

Glossopteris

Massospondylus

Continental jigsaw
The shapes of the continents fit together like a giant jigsaw. This may be the most obvious evidence that the continents were once linked.

▨ PRECAMBRIAN ROCK
▨ PALEOZOIC ROCK

Exploration

PEOPLE HAVE SAILED the seas for thousands of years in search of new homes, better trade routes, and adventure. But the detailed study of the oceans only really began in 1872, with the voyage of HMS *Challenger*. Its crew spent more than three years investigating all aspects of the oceans – their chemistry, physics, and biology. The reports written by *Challenger*'s scientists form the basis of the modern science of oceanography – the scientific study of the oceans. Modern technology has helped further this knowledge. Scientists can now investigate deeper than ever before. The latest submersibles (small, free-swimming, underwater vehicles) and ROVs (remote-operated vehicles) are expanding our knowledge of the oceans, and new discoveries are being made all the time.

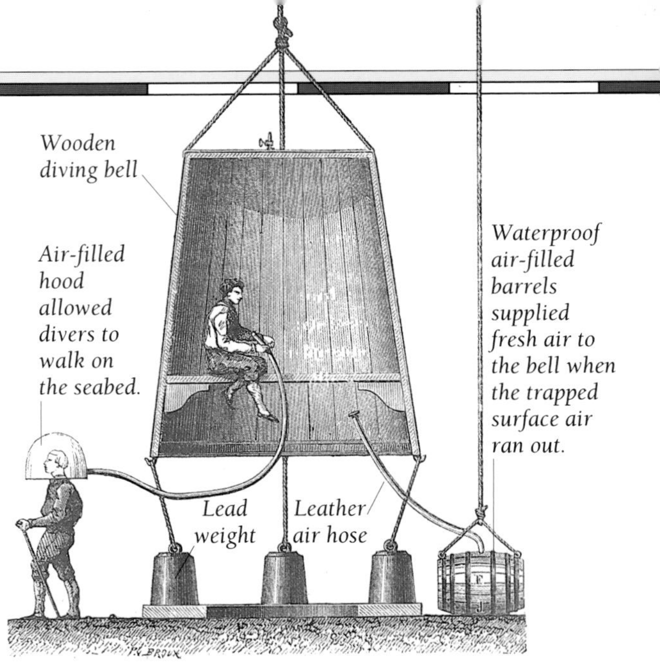

EXPLORATION TODAY

Until recently scientists had very little idea about what the ocean floor looked like. After 1945, however, major advances were made in exploration techniques. The greatest steps forward came in the 1960s with the development of modern submersibles and unmanned ROVs. Both operate from research and support ships on the surface. Some of the newer equipment, such as GLORIA, shown below, has been developed by the U.K.'s Institute of Oceanographic Sciences.

MAPPING WITH SOUND

Scientists use sonar (sound) to make maps of the deep-sea floor, indicating features such as volcanoes and trenches. Sonar instruments give out pulses of sound. These hit parts of the seabed and send back echoes. The echoes are recorded, and their pattern traced on paper to build up a "sound image" of the features.

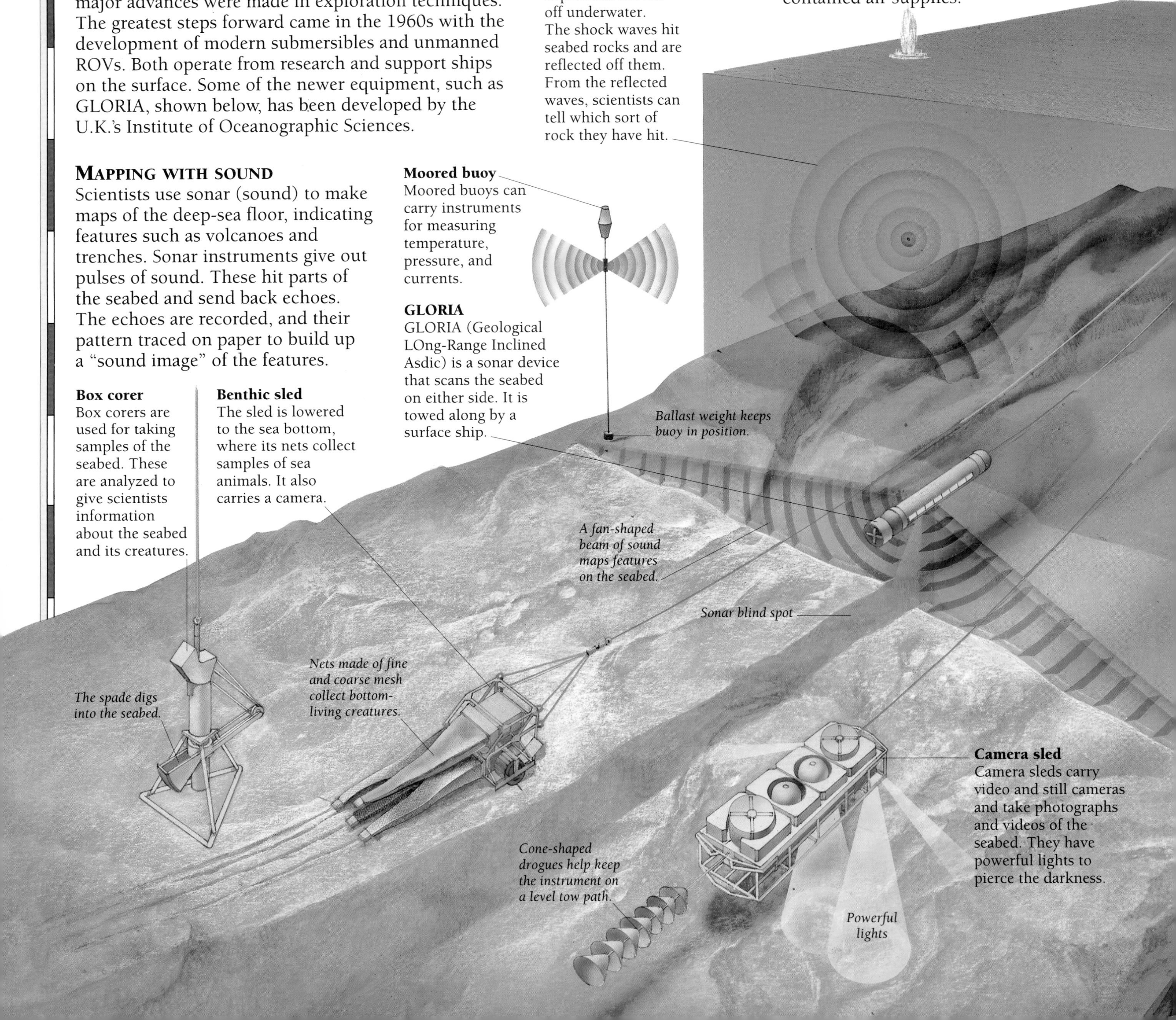

Box corer
Box corers are used for taking samples of the seabed. These are analyzed to give scientists information about the seabed and its creatures.

Benthic sled
The sled is lowered to the sea bottom, where its nets collect samples of sea animals. It also carries a camera.

Seismic profiling
To explore for oil, explosions are set off underwater. The shock waves hit seabed rocks and are reflected off them. From the reflected waves, scientists can tell which sort of rock they have hit.

Moored buoy
Moored buoys can carry instruments for measuring temperature, pressure, and currents.

GLORIA
GLORIA (Geological LOng-Range Inclined Asdic) is a sonar device that scans the seabed on either side. It is towed along by a surface ship.

Ballast weight keeps buoy in position.

A fan-shaped beam of sound maps features on the seabed.

Sonar blind spot

The spade digs into the seabed.

Nets made of fine and coarse mesh collect bottom-living creatures.

Cone-shaped drogues help keep the instrument on a level tow path.

Camera sled
Camera sleds carry video and still cameras and take photographs and videos of the seabed. They have powerful lights to pierce the darkness.

Powerful lights

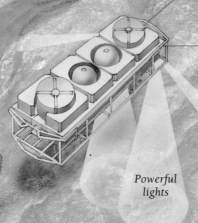

Wooden diving bell

Air-filled hood allowed divers to walk on the seabed.

Waterproof air-filled barrels supplied fresh air to the bell when the trapped surface air ran out.

Lead weight

Leather air hose

HALLEY'S DIVING BELL

The astronomer Sir Edmond Halley built his famous "diving bell" in 1690. It allowed divers to work on the seabed. Air was trapped inside the bell at the surface and was used by the divers below. Diving bells are still used today, but with modern self-contained air supplies.

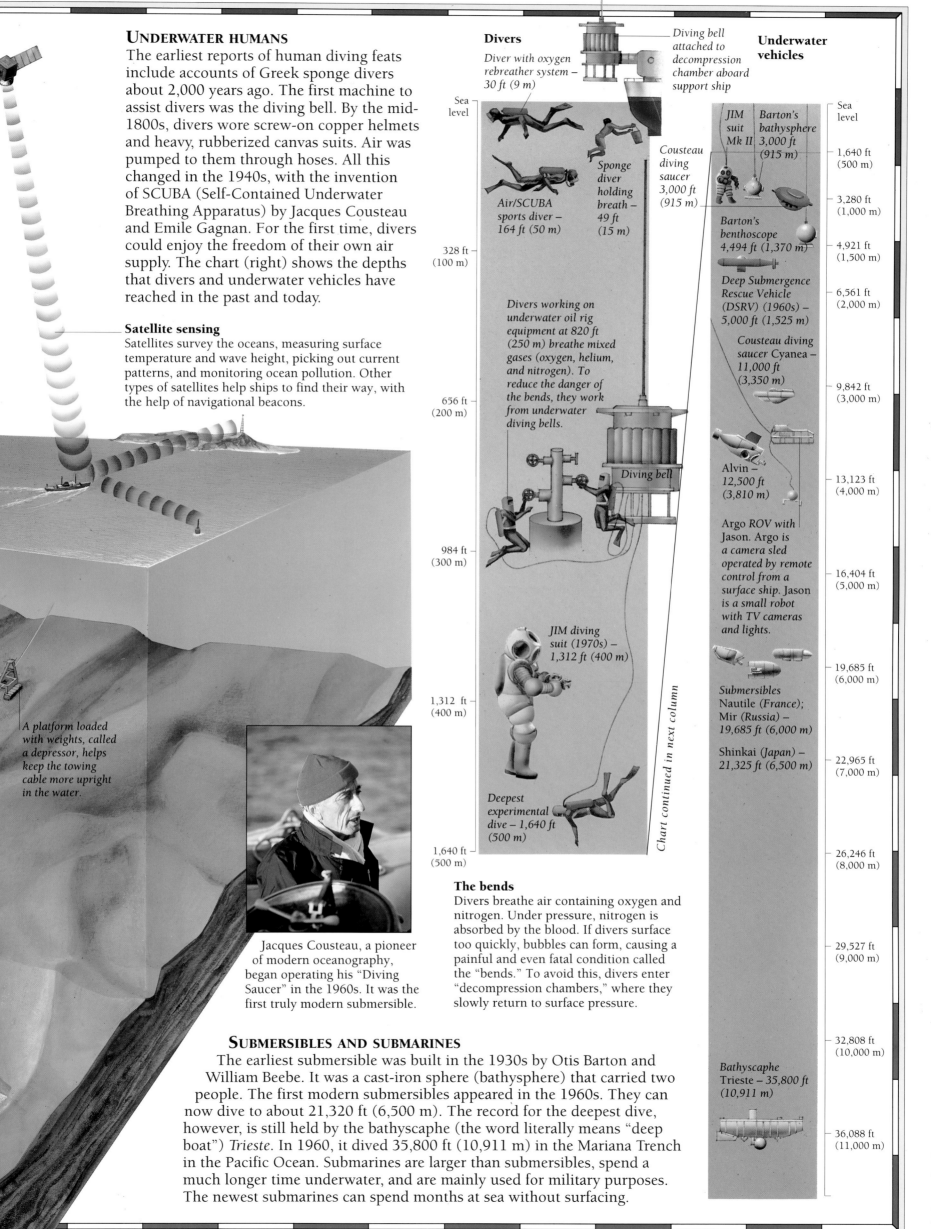

UNDERWATER HUMANS

The earliest reports of human diving feats include accounts of Greek sponge divers about 2,000 years ago. The first machine to assist divers was the diving bell. By the mid-1800s, divers wore screw-on copper helmets and heavy, rubberized canvas suits. Air was pumped to them through hoses. All this changed in the 1940s, with the invention of SCUBA (Self-Contained Underwater Breathing Apparatus) by Jacques Cousteau and Emile Gagnan. For the first time, divers could enjoy the freedom of their own air supply. The chart (right) shows the depths that divers and underwater vehicles have reached in the past and today.

Satellite sensing

Satellites survey the oceans, measuring surface temperature and wave height, picking out current patterns, and monitoring ocean pollution. Other types of satellites help ships to find their way, with the help of navigational beacons.

A platform loaded with weights, called a depressor, helps keep the towing cable more upright in the water.

Jacques Cousteau, a pioneer of modern oceanography, began operating his "Diving Saucer" in the 1960s. It was the first truly modern submersible.

SUBMERSIBLES AND SUBMARINES

The earliest submersible was built in the 1930s by Otis Barton and William Beebe. It was a cast-iron sphere (bathysphere) that carried two people. The first modern submersibles appeared in the 1960s. They can now dive to about 21,320 ft (6,500 m). The record for the deepest dive, however, is still held by the bathyscaphe (the word literally means "deep boat") *Trieste*. In 1960, it dived 35,800 ft (10,911 m) in the Mariana Trench in the Pacific Ocean. Submarines are larger than submersibles, spend a much longer time underwater, and are mainly used for military purposes. The newest submarines can spend months at sea without surfacing.

Divers

Diver with oxygen rebreather system – 30 ft (9 m)

Diving bell attached to decompression chamber aboard support ship

Underwater vehicles

Sea level

Air/SCUBA sports diver – 164 ft (50 m)

Sponge diver holding breath – 49 ft (15 m)

Cousteau diving saucer 3,000 ft (915 m)

328 ft (100 m)

Divers working on underwater oil rig equipment at 820 ft (250 m) breathe mixed gases (oxygen, helium, and nitrogen). To reduce the danger of the bends, they work from underwater diving bells.

656 ft (200 m)

984 ft (300 m)

Diving bell

JIM diving suit (1970s) – 1,312 ft (400 m)

1,312 ft (400 m)

Deepest experimental dive – 1,640 ft (500 m)

1,640 ft (500 m)

Chart continued in next column

JIM suit Mk II

Barton's bathysphere 3,000 ft (915 m)

Sea level

1,640 ft (500 m)

3,280 ft (1,000 m)

Barton's benthoscope 4,494 ft (1,370 m)

4,921 ft (1,500 m)

Deep Submergence Rescue Vehicle (DSRV) (1960s) – 5,000 ft (1,525 m)

6,561 ft (2,000 m)

Cousteau diving saucer Cyanea – 11,000 ft (3,350 m)

9,842 ft (3,000 m)

Alvin – 12,500 ft (3,810 m)

13,123 ft (4,000 m)

Argo ROV with Jason. Argo is a camera sled operated by remote control from a surface ship. Jason is a small robot with TV cameras and lights.

16,404 ft (5,000 m)

19,685 ft (6,000 m)

Submersibles Nautile (France); Mir (Russia) – 19,685 ft (6,000 m)

Shinkai (Japan) – 21,325 ft (6,500 m)

22,965 ft (7,000 m)

26,246 ft (8,000 m)

29,527 ft (9,000 m)

32,808 ft (10,000 m)

Bathyscaphe Trieste – 35,800 ft (10,911 m)

36,088 ft (11,000 m)

The bends

Divers breathe air containing oxygen and nitrogen. Under pressure, nitrogen is absorbed by the blood. If divers surface too quickly, bubbles can form, causing a painful and even fatal condition called the "bends." To avoid this, divers enter "decompression chambers," where they slowly return to surface pressure.

The Web of Life

THE OCEANS FORM THE LARGEST environment for living things on Earth. A huge variety of plants and animals live in the sea – both in the surface water and at every depth. As on land, they are linked together by what they eat. Every ocean food chain begins with marine plants because of the plants' ability to photosynthesize. This is the process by which plants use the energy from sunlight to combine water and carbon dioxide into food. In a simple food chain, the plants are eaten by herbivores (plant-eaters), which, in turn, are eaten by carnivores (meat-eaters). But food chains are rarely simple. They are usually linked to create the more complex food webs shown below in which the plants and animals are dependent on each other. If one link is destroyed, the rest of the web is affected.

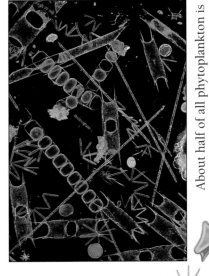

THE LIGHTED REALM
Most sea animals live in the top 500 ft (150 m) of the sea, in the lighted, or euphotic, zone. The water is warm and sunny here and plants can grow in abundance. Three areas make up the euphotic zone – estuaries, rocky coasts, and the open ocean.

MARINE PLANTS
By far the most abundant plants in the sea are the microscopic, single-celled phytoplankton which drift on the surface of the water. They are algae, the simplest types of plant. Larger algae grow along the shore and in shallow water. These are the seaweeds, the biggest of which can grow to more than 164 ft (50 m) in length. There are relatively few flowering plants living in or near the sea. Among them are seagrasses and mangroves.

About half of all phytoplankton is made up of microscopic diatoms (shown magnified many times above). There may be a million of these tiny plants in one quart (one liter) of seawater.

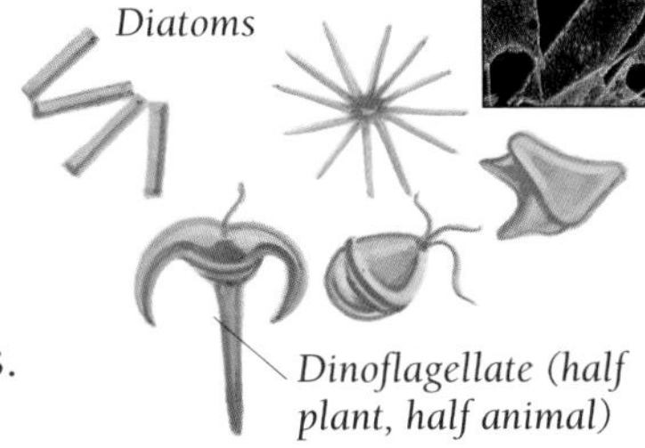

Diatoms

Dinoflagellate (half plant, half animal)

HERBIVORES AND CARNIVORES
In the first part of a simple food chain, the phytoplankton is eaten by tiny herbivores, the zooplankton. They, in turn, are eaten by carnivores, which fall prey to larger carnivores, and so on. In the second part of the chain, the dead bodies and waste from the animals higher up sink and are fed upon by the decomposers (waste-eaters).

Rocky coasts
Seaweeds grow well along rocky coasts and provide food for large numbers of grazing animals, which include small snails and sea urchins. Other creatures, such as barnacles and sea squirts, feed on the phytoplankton. Some coastal seabirds have beaks specially adapted for prying open mollusks.

Periwinkles
Periwinkles and other small snails are eaten by seabirds such as gulls and oystercatchers.

Barnacles
When submerged, barnacles extend their long feathery feeding arms in search of food.

Snail tales
Periwinkles feed on bladder wrack and other sea plants, while snails such as whelks feed on barnacles and periwinkles.

Life in estuaries
Estuaries form where rivers meet the sea. Some of an estuary's food supply is made up of plant debris washed off the land by the rivers. At low tide, an estuary may look lifeless, but there are hundreds of animals hidden in the mud. They provide food for seabirds such as gulls and plovers.

Plants in the sea
Phytoplankton cannot grow below about 500 ft (150 m) because there is no sunlight for photosynthesis. On the surface, however, the phytoplankton may drift in vast numbers.

Pass the debris
Shore worms and small snails eat debris in the soft mud.

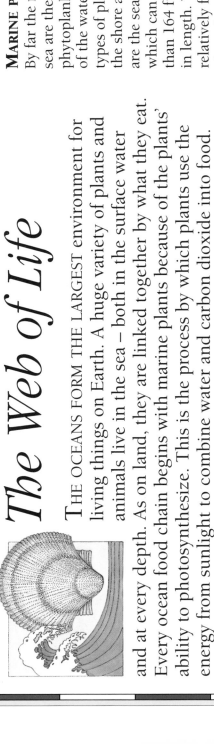

Plant debris washes off the land into the mud.

Shore crab

Ragworm

Cockle

Ringed plover

Lugworm

Herring gull

Oystercatcher

Sea squirts

Toothy grin
Wolf fish eat sea urchins, which they crush with their large teeth.

Bladder wrack

Sea urchin

Dog whelk

Oarweed

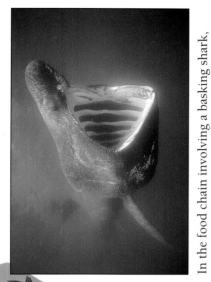

In the food chain involving a basking shark, several links are bypassed. The shark feeds directly on zooplankton which it filters from the water. It filters more than 330,000 gallons (1.5 million liters) of water an hour as it feeds.

THE GREAT PYRAMID OF LIFE

An example of one single food chain shows just how many individual creatures are consumed by others in the ocean every day. One humpback whale needs to eat about 5,000 herring to feel full. Each herring may have eaten 6,000–7,000 small crustaceans, such as shrimps. Each shrimp may have eaten as many as 130,000 diatoms. This means that it takes some 4 billion diatoms to provide one whale with an average meal.

4 billion diatoms

30 million small crustaceans

5,000 herring

1 humpback whale

At each step in a food chain, a large amount of energy is lost. As a result, each link in the chain is larger in size and less numerous than the one before, creating a food pyramid.

The open ocean

Out in the open ocean, microscopic phytoplankton are the only source of plant food. They are grazed on by tiny zooplankton such as copepods, which in turn feed larger fish and other carnivores. Fast-swimming hunters, such as killer whales and tuna, are highly successful open-ocean predators.

Zooplankton

The phytoplankton (plant plankton) are eaten by tiny sea animals called zooplankton. Some hide in the depths of the sea during the day and migrate to the surface at night to feed.

Copepod

Herring

Herring and other fish eat huge quantities of copepods.

Porpoise

The herrings may be caught and eaten by porpoises, which, in turn, may fall prey to hungry killer whales.

THE DARK REALM

Below about 3,280 ft (1,000 m) the sea is permanently dark. No sunlight can penetrate the water and no plants can grow. Many deep-sea animals rely on a "rain" of dead plant and animal bodies or wastes from the surface. Although some of this material is eaten on its way down, a surprising amount reaches the bottom of the sea and nourishes an amazing variety of creatures.

Sediment life

Microscopic organisms, bacteria, small worms, and crustaceans are filtered from the sediment by many bottom-living creatures.

Burrowing urchins

Heart urchins burrow into the sea-bed, feeding on tiny creatures hidden in the sediment.

Seabed suns

Sunstars are members of the starfish family. They are predators, feeding on various forms of bottom life.

Five-arm feeders

Brittle stars feed on dead organic matter suspended in the water.

Fishy predators

Cod are predators and scavengers, feeding on both smaller fish and dead organic matter.

Cucumber meal

Sea cucumbers feed on food from the surface of the seafloor.

COD EAT HERRING

HERRING EAT ZOOPLANKTON

Dead matter sinks to the seafloor

COD EAT SEA CUCUMBERS

PORPOISES EAT COD

SUNSTARS EAT BRITTLE STARS

The Atlantic Ocean

THE ATLANTIC OCEAN is the world's second largest ocean, after the Pacific. It covers an area of about 31,660,446 sq miles (82,000,000 sq km) – about one-fifth of the Earth's surface. It stretches from the Arctic Ocean in the north to the Antarctic Ocean in the south. Its western boundary is formed by the continents of North and South America, and its eastern boundary by Europe and Africa. At its widest point, it measures 5,965 miles (9,600 km). But it is still spreading sideward at a rate of ¾–1½ in (2–4 cm) a year along the Mid-Atlantic Ridge, the great underwater mountain range that splits the ocean down the middle. The ocean is divided into the North and South Atlantic areas by the Equator. The Atlantic is a relatively young ocean, only about 150 million years old. It has an average depth of 12,000 ft (3,660 m) and is 28,374 ft (8,648 m) deep at its deepest point.

Continental shelf

The continental shelf is the shallow area next to the land. In the Atlantic, it is a large source of fish and minerals. About 90 percent of all the fish caught for food come from the continental shelves. There are important fisheries off the coast of eastern Canada and northwestern Europe. There are also large deposits of minerals, such as oil, gas, gravel, and shell sand. But the shelf area is being polluted by sewage, oil, chemicals, and debris, especially around built-up areas on the east coast of the United States, such as New York.

Puerto Rico Trench

The Puerto Rico Trench is the deepest point in the Atlantic, at 28,374 ft (8,648 m). It lies to the north of Puerto Rico and is the result of movement between the Caribbean and American plates.

North Atlantic Ocean

The North Atlantic stretches from the tropical Equator to the icebound Arctic. In the north, high winds, waves, fog, and icebergs can make conditions hazardous for ships. The North Atlantic is bordered by some of the world's most industrialized countries and is one of the busiest areas for shipping. It also has some of the world's richest fishing grounds along its continental shelves. More than 3 million tons (3.1 million tonnes) of fish are caught there each year.

Many of the icebergs seen in the North Atlantic have broken off from the ice sheet that covers Greenland. This breaking-off process is called "calving." The bergs are then carried south by the current.

The *Titanic* was the largest ship of its time and thought to be unsinkable. Here it leaves its builders, Harland and Wolff of Belfast, Northern Ireland, in 1912.

DISCOVERING THE *TITANIC*

On April 14, 1912, the luxury ocean liner *Titanic* hit an iceberg in the North Atlantic and sank. Nearly 1,500 people died in the tragedy. The wreck was discovered 73 years later by an expedition led by Dr. Robert Ballard. A towed camera system, *Argo*, spotted it at 13,123 ft (4,000 m) at the base of the continental shelf, as indicated below.

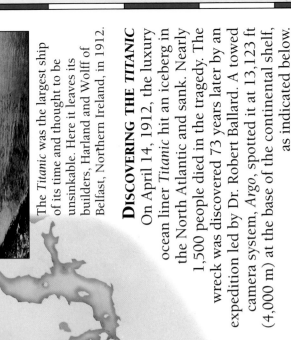

NEWFOUNDLAND

Site of the sunken wreck of the Titanic

GREENLAND

LABRADOR

NEWFOUNDLAND

CONTINENTAL SHELF

ICELAND

REYKJANES RIDGE

Faeroe Islands

BRITISH ISLES

IRELAND

EUROPE

AFRICA

B

CONTINENTAL SHELF

MID-ATLANTIC RIDGE

Azores

Site of project FAMOUS exploration

Canary Islands

Cape Verde Islands

LINE OF CROSS-SECTION

Site where the *Titanic* was discovered.

NORTH AMERICA

CENTRAL AMERICA

Cuba

Hispaniola

WEST INDIES

Puerto Rico

SOUTH

Mid-Atlantic Ridge

The Mid-Atlantic Ridge runs for some 7,000 miles (11,300 km) down the middle of the Atlantic Ocean, from north of Iceland to Bouvet Island on the edge of the Antarctic Ocean. Most of the ridge lies underwater, but it rises to the surface in Iceland and Ascension Island. Along the ridge, molten rock seeps up from deep inside the Earth and creates new seabed rock.

This photograph was taken from the submersible *Alvin*. It shows newly formed lava on the Mid-Atlantic Ridge.

SOUTH ATLANTIC OCEAN

The South Atlantic Ocean stretches from the warm water of the tropics to the cold waters of the Antarctic Ocean. It is the site of some of the most isolated islands in the world. Bouvet Island lies 1,050 miles (1,700 km) off the east coast of Antarctica. Tristan da Cunha is the world's most isolated inhabited island. Its people's nearest neighbors live on St. Helena, 1,300 miles (2,120 km) away.

On the shelf

The continental margin is made up of the continental shelf, slope, and rise. The margin is wider in the Atlantic than in the Pacific. The Atlantic shelf alone is up to 932 miles (1,500 km) wide, although it narrows along the west coast of Africa. The slope is up to 62 miles (100 km) wide.

Magnificent mountains

The mountains that make up the Mid-Atlantic Ridge are up to 13,123 ft (4,000 m) high. Their tips lie about 6,561 ft (2,000 m) below the sea. Part of the ridge was studied intensively by the FAMOUS (French-American Mid-Ocean Underwater Study) project in the 1970s.

Caribbean Sea

The Caribbean Sea covers an area of about 1,019,311 sq miles (2,640,000 sq km). Its deepest point is the Cayman Trench, at 25,216 ft (7,686 m). The sea is bordered in the east and west by subduction zones. About 14 percent of the world's coral reefs are found in the Caribbean Sea.

ATLANTIC CROSS-SECTION

The chart below shows a cross-section through the Atlantic from Central America to Africa between points A–B, marked on the map above.

Massive migrations

The Sargasso Sea is the spawning ground of the remarkable European and American eels. Every autumn the adult eels leave their river homes and swim across the Atlantic to the Sargasso Sea. They gather in the millions to lay their eggs deep in the water, then they die. The young eels, or elvers, drift on the ocean currents back to the same rivers their parents came from. The journey takes two years for the European eels and one year for the American eels.

THE SARGASSO SEA

The Sargasso Sea is a huge area of calm, still water in the western North Atlantic. It is famous for the green-brown weed, called sargassum weed (right), which covers its surface. Portuguese sailors named the sea after a type of grape, because the air-filled bladders that keep it afloat look like grapes. The sea is home to some unique animals, including fish and crabs that are camouflaged to blend in with the weed.

Common eel

Undersea earthquakes often rumble through the Sandwich Trench region.

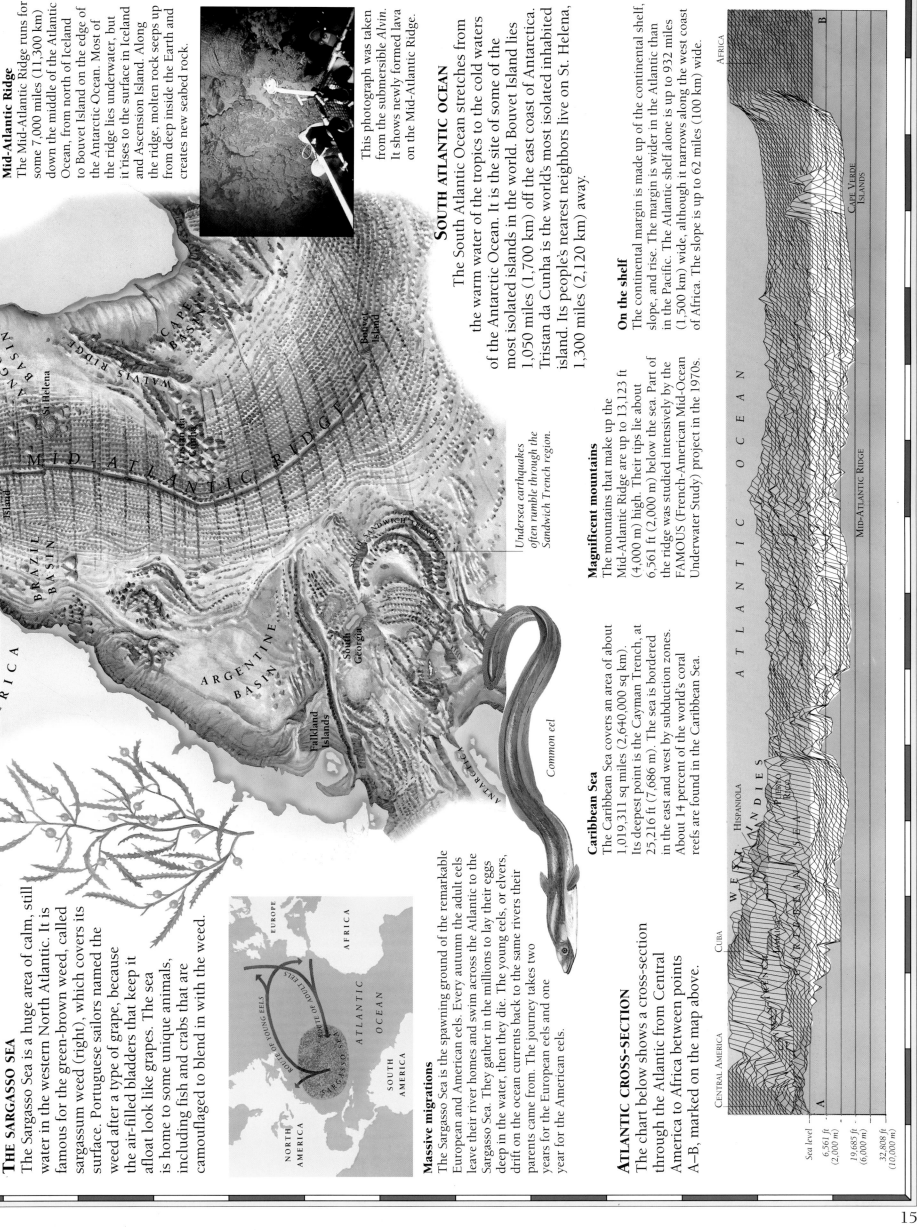

Route of young eels
Route of adult eels

EUROPE
AFRICA
NORTH AMERICA
SOUTH AMERICA
ATLANTIC OCEAN
SARGASSO SEA

ANGOLA BASIN
CAPE BASIN
WALVIS RIDGE
St Helena
Bouvet Island
Tristan da Cunha
Ascension Island
MID-ATLANTIC RIDGE
BRAZIL BASIN
SOUTH SANDWICH TRENCH
ARGENTINE BASIN
South Georgia
Falkland Islands
ANTARCTICA
AMERICA

AFRICA
B
ATLANTIC OCEAN
CAPE VERDE ISLANDS
MID-ATLANTIC RIDGE
CENTRAL AMERICA
CUBA
HISPANIOLA
PUERTO RICO
WEST INDIES
CARIBBEAN SEA
PUERTO RICO TRENCH
A
Sea level
6,561 ft (2,000 m)
19,685 ft (6,000 m)
32,808 ft (10,000 m)

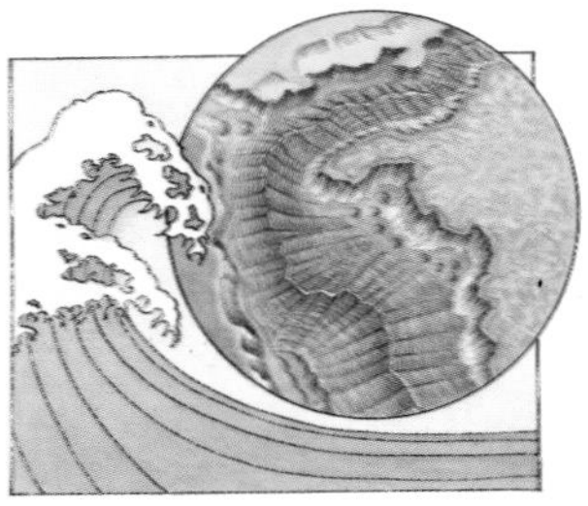

Continental Margins

AROUND THE EDGES OF THE CONTINENTS, the land slopes from the shore into the deep sea. These coastal areas are called continental margins. A margin is usually made up of three parts – the continental shelf, the continental slope, and the continental rise. Each varies in width, steepness, and depth around the different continents.

There are two basic types of continental margins, called Atlantic and Pacific, although they do not only occur in these two oceans. Atlantic-type margins, such as the one around northern Europe shown here, have broad continental shelves and rises. The continent and seafloor form part of the same crustal plate so there is little or no volcanic or earthquake (seismic) activity. Pacific-type margins have narrow shelves, steep slopes, and deep trenches in place of continental rises. The continent and seafloor are on different plates. There is lots of seismic activity because the seafloor is subducted under the continent.

Atlantic margins
This map shows the continental shelf around northern Europe. The shelf is wide, like those in all Atlantic-type margins. The picture below shows the same region, but looking towards the British Isles from the mid-Atlantic. The arrow on this map shows the viewpoint for the main picture.

Continental shelf
The continental shelf slopes gently out to sea, like a huge shelf of submerged land. On average, shelves are 43 miles (70 km) wide. Off the north coast of Siberia, however, the shelf reaches a width of 559 miles (900 km). The edge of a shelf is marked by a steeper slope, called the shelf break.

Continental slope
The continental slope reaches from the shelf break to the continental rise. It is steeper, deeper, and narrower than the shelf, ending about 8,200 ft (2,500 m) below the surface, and with an average width of 12 miles (20 km). The slope is often cut by submarine canyons.

Continental rise
The continental rise is a thick wedge of sediment (sand and mud) which stretches from the slope down to the deep-sea floor, more than 13,123 ft (4,000 m) below the surface. The sediment is carried down from the continental shelf and slope by underwater avalanches called turbidity currents.

The diagram below shows the continental shelf, slope, and rise on a typical Atlantic margin, and the biological zones that correspond to them.

This rat-tail fish was photographed on the continental slope in the Porcupine Seabight.

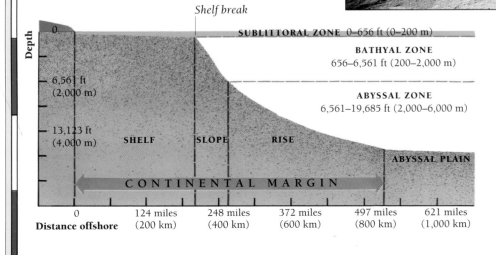

SUBLITTORAL ZONE 0–656 ft (0–200 m)

BATHYAL ZONE 656–6,561 ft (200–2,000 m)

ABYSSAL ZONE 6,561–19,685 ft (2,000–6,000 m)

Depth

0

6,561 ft (2,000 m)

13,123 ft (4,000 m)

Shelf break

SHELF   SLOPE   RISE

ABYSSAL PLAIN

CONTINENTAL MARGIN

| Distance offshore | 0 | 124 miles (200 km) | 248 miles (400 km) | 372 miles (600 km) | 497 miles (800 km) | 621 miles (1,000 km) |

ZONES OF LIFE
Scientists divide the ocean into a number of depth zones (see diagram on the left). These zones roughly match the physical features of the continental margin. The sublittoral zone corresponds to the continental shelf; the bathyal zone corresponds to the slope; and the abyssal zone corresponds to the rise and abyssal plain beyond. Different creatures live in each of these zones. The deeper you go, the fewer creatures there are because there is less food to live on, and conditions are more difficult – it is colder, darker, and the pressure is crushing.

SUBMARINE CANYONS

Submarine canyons are huge, deep valleys cut into the floor of the continental margin. Eroded and widened by avalanches of water and sediment, they start life on the continental shelf, often at the point where a large river runs into the sea. Many submarine canyons are V-shaped, like river valleys on land. They may be more than 3,280 ft (1,000 m) deep. The canyons act as passageways for loads of sediment that continue to flow down the continental slope into the deep sea.

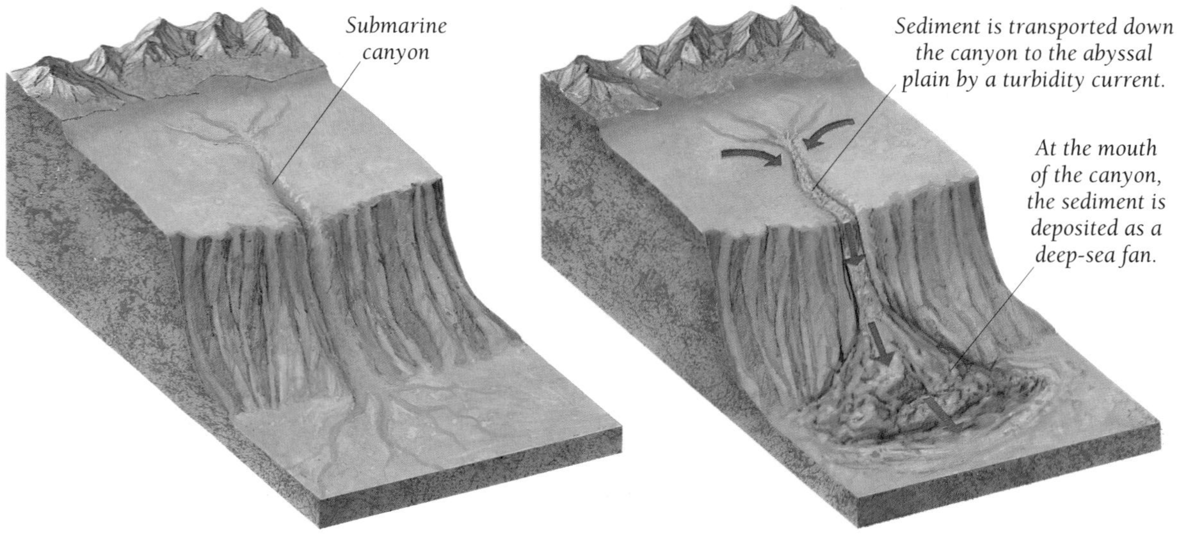

Submarine canyon

Sediment is transported down the canyon to the abyssal plain by a turbidity current.

At the mouth of the canyon, the sediment is deposited as a deep-sea fan.

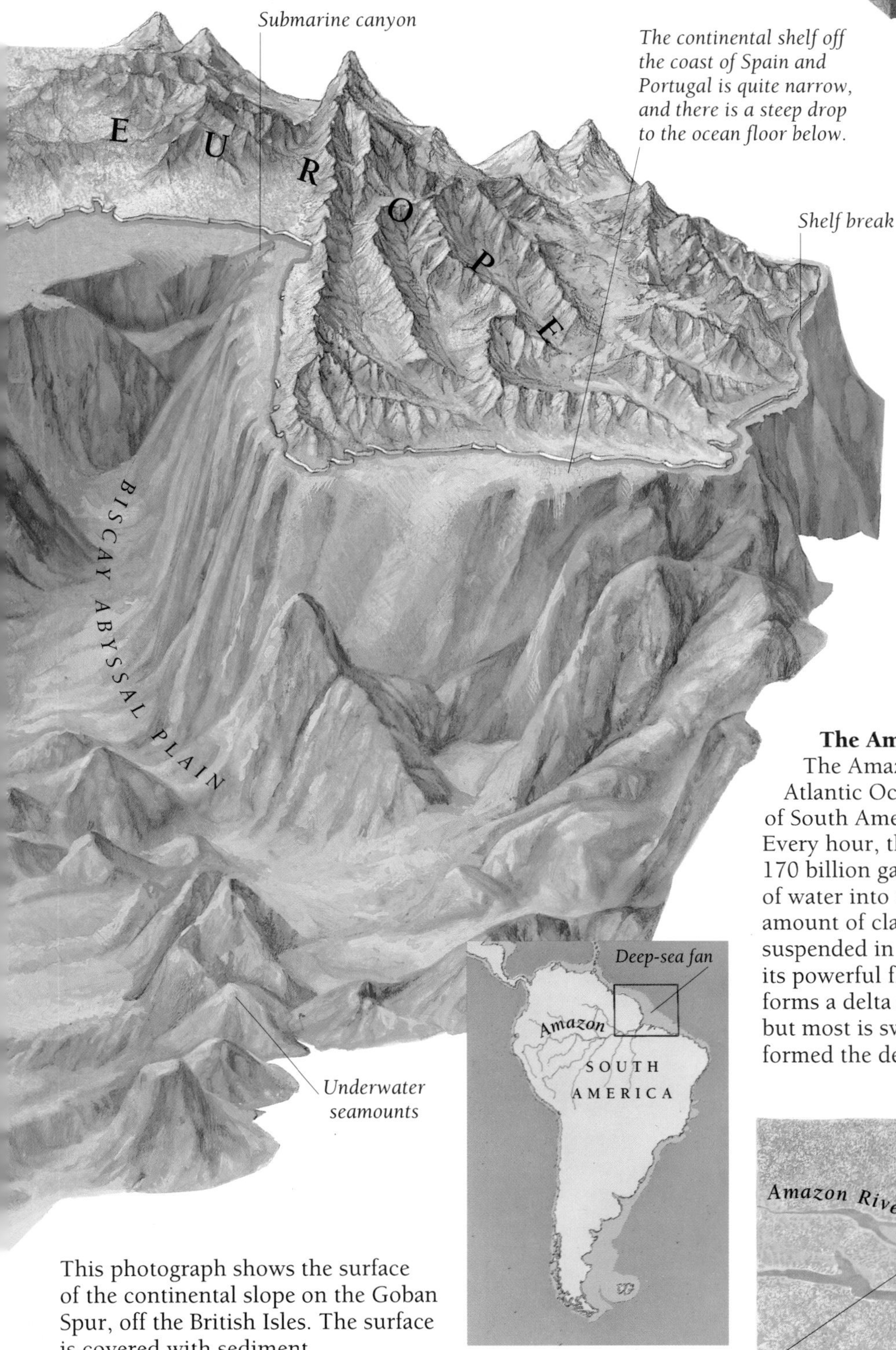

Submarine canyon

The continental shelf off the coast of Spain and Portugal is quite narrow, and there is a steep drop to the ocean floor below.

Shelf break

E U R O P E

B I S C A Y   A B Y S S A L   P L A I N

TURBIDITY CURRENTS

Turbidity currents are underwater avalanches of water and mud that carry huge quantities of sediment from the continental shelf down the continental slope. They may be triggered by earthquakes, floods, or other disturbances. At first, these currents flow very quickly, sometimes with such speed and power that they have been known to snap underwater cables in two. As the slope gets gentler, the currents slow down and deposit their load on the deep-sea floor.

DEEP-SEA FANS

Deep-sea fans form at the bottom of submarine canyons, where a turbidity current deposits its load of sediment. The sediment spreads out in a wide fan shape on the relatively flat seafloor. These fans are only found on Atlantic-style continental margins. On a Pacific-style margin, where there is a trench next to the continental slope, the sediment is deposited into the trench and a fan cannot form.

The Amazon fan

The Amazon River flows into the Atlantic Ocean on the northeast coast of South America (see map on the left). Every hour, the Amazon pours about 170 billion gallons (773 billion liters) of water into the Atlantic. A massive amount of clay, mud, and silt is suspended in the water, carried along by its powerful flow. Some of this sediment forms a delta at the mouth of the river, but most is swept out to sea, and has formed the deep-sea fan shown below.

In this aerial view of part of the Amazon delta, the gray areas are deposits of sediment. Other sediment is washed out over the continental shelf and eventually forms a deep-sea fan.

Underwater seamounts

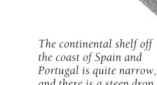

Deep-sea fan

Amazon

SOUTH AMERICA

This photograph shows the surface of the continental slope on the Goban Spur, off the British Isles. The surface is covered with sediment.

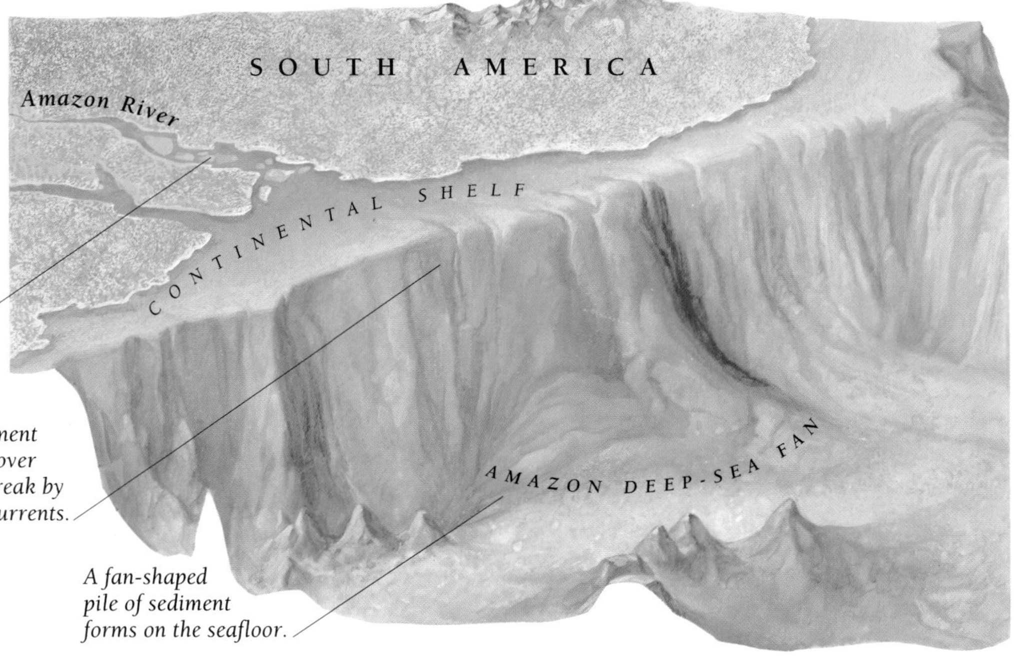

Sediment is carried into the ocean from the Amazon River.

Some sediment is washed over the shelf break by turbidity currents.

A fan-shaped pile of sediment forms on the seafloor.

S O U T H   A M E R I C A

Amazon River

C O N T I N E N T A L   S H E L F

A M A Z O N   D E E P - S E A   F A N

Abyssal Plains

THE ABYSSAL PLAINS begin where the continental margins end. They are found at depths of 13,123–19,685 ft (4,000–6,000 m) below the surface of the sea. Only the deep-sea trenches plunge farther down. The abyssal plains are not only the flattest but also the most featureless places on Earth. Many of the hills and hollows in the underlying seabed crust were buried long ago under the thick layer of sediment that carpets the plains. The gradient (or steepness) of the plains is only 1:1,000. This means that for every one mile (1.6 km) you walked, you would only climb a slope 5 ft 2 in (1.6 m) high.

Until about a hundred years ago, no one believed that anything could live on the abyssal plains. We now know differently. Modern research has shown that, despite the pitch-blackness of the water, the freezing cold, and the crushing pressure, some amazing and bizarre creatures have adapted to life in the depths of the sea.

Where abyssal plains are found
Abyssal plains cover almost half of the deep-sea floor. They lie between the edges of the continental margins and the mid-ocean ridges, and are 125–1,250 miles (200–2,000 km) wide. Abyssal plains exist in all of the oceans, but are more common in the Atlantic and Indian Oceans and quite rare in the Pacific. The shaded areas on the map above show the location of the major abyssal plains.

Halosaur
The halosaur is another type of bottom-dwelling fish. It is about 6 ft 6 in (2 m) long, with a sharply pointed snout and a tapering body. The halosaur is thought to use its snout to dislodge invertebrates from the seabed. It also eats deep-sea squid.

THE ABYSSAL BENTHOS
The "abyssal benthos" is the term used to describe the animals that live in, on, or close to the deep-sea floor of the abyssal plains. The vast majority of these creatures live buried in the sediment, hidden from view. They range from tiny, single-celled animals to larger worms and shrimps. Other animals, such as starfish, sea cucumbers, and sea urchins, live on the surface of the seafloor. A few creatures can swim up off the bottom. These include deep-sea shrimps, prawns, and some extraordinary fish.

Tripod fish
The tripod fish gets its name from the three extra-long fins extending from its body. It uses these like stilts to stand on the bottom, keeping its body just above the surface of the seafloor. Then it sits and waits to ambush any passing prey. When the prey comes within range, the tripod fish pounces on it.

Venus flower basket (type of glass sponge)

Swimming tripod fish

Sea cucumber

Tripod fish standing on seafloor

Glass sponges
Tulip-shaped glass sponges grow to about 16 in (40 cm) high and are raised off the seafloor by long stalks of twisted silica. The silica "skeletons" are just like fiberglass.

Starfish
The echinoderms are the most common group of larger animals found on the abyssal plains. They include sea urchins, sea cucumbers, brittle stars, and starfish. The word "echinoderm" means "spiny skinned."

Sea cucumber
Despite the fact that they are soft and slimy, sea cucumbers are echinoderms like starfish. These creatures flourish on the abyssal plains. Most sea cucumbers crawl slowly across the deep-sea floor, feeding on the remains of animals and plants found in the mud and ooze. This is called detritus feeding.

Giant sea spider
The giant sea spider is found at depths of about 16,404 ft (5,000 m). It moves over the soft ooze of the deep-sea bed on its very long legs. It feeds on the juices of worms and other soft-bodied invertebrates, which it sucks out with its proboscis (feeding tube).

ABYSSOPELAGIC ANIMALS

Creatures that live in the water above the abyssal plains are known as "abyssopelagic" animals. This group includes some remarkable fish, squid, and prawns. The fish are almost always black, for camouflage. They are usually carnivores, with huge mouths armed with sharp teeth, and stretchy stomachs. These enable them to take full advantage of any food they are lucky enough to find, even if their prey is two or three times larger than they are.

Halosaur

SEEING IN THE DARK

Many of the fish that live in the dark sea depths make their own light. They do this either by means of special chemicals, called luciferins, or through luminous bacteria that live in their bodies. The fish use light to attract prey and to identify one another.

Gulper eel

The gulper eel has huge, pouchlike jaws. These can open wide enough, and its stomach stretch far enough, for it to swallow fish much bigger than itself.

The gulper eel (left) can unhinge its jaws, opening its cavernous mouth even wider.

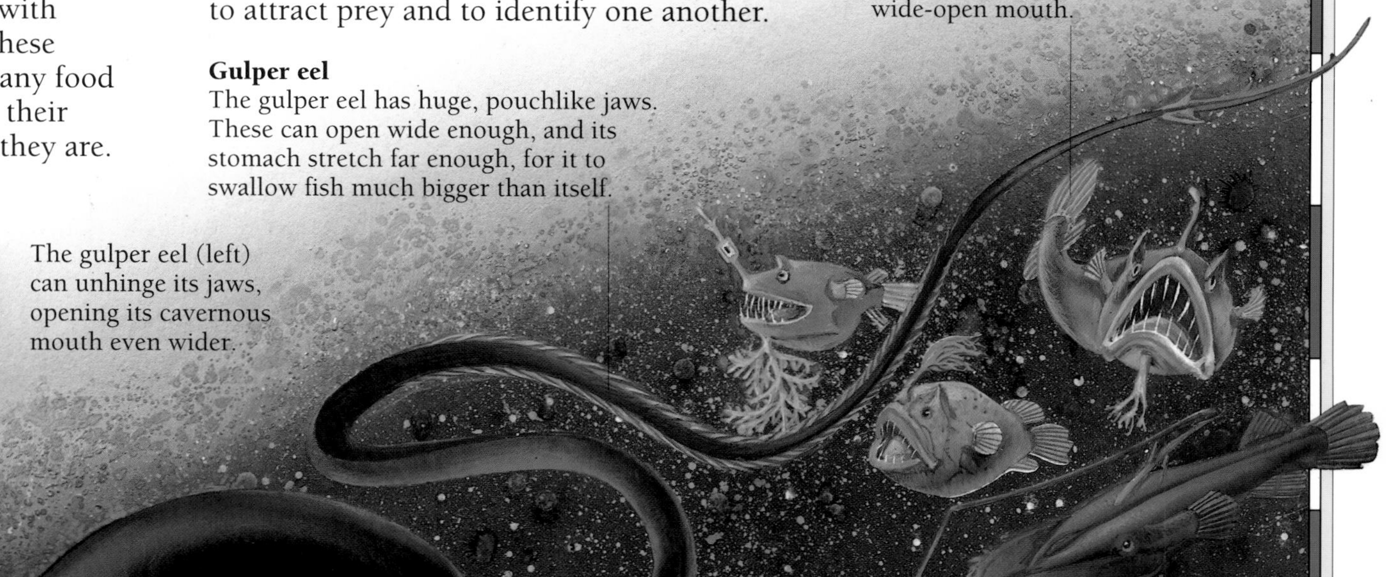

Angler fish

The deep-sea angler fish has a long fishing-rod fin hanging down over its mouth, with a blob of light at the end. Small fish mistake the light for food and swim straight toward it – right into the angler fish's huge, wide-open mouth.

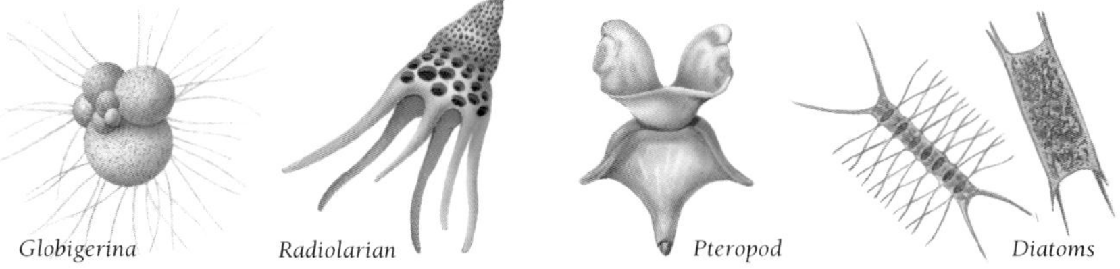

TRACKS IN THE SAND

As animals move about over the abyssal plain, they leave a crisscross of marks or tracks behind. These marks are called *Lebensspuren*, which is German for "traces of life." It can take a long time for them to be covered by sediment and disappear.

Sea urchin

Brittle star

Sea pen

Sea pens are soft corals, related to stony, reef-building corals. They are named after old-fashioned quill pens. Sea pens can reach a height of 5 ft (1.5 m).

SEABED SEDIMENTS

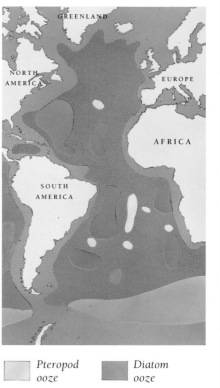

The layer of sediment that carpets the plains is usually 984–1,640 ft (300–500 m) thick. This map shows the different types of sediment that are found in the Atlantic Ocean. The sediment has taken millions of years to accumulate, at a rate of less than ½ in (or 1–15 mm) every thousand years. Some of it has been washed into the sea from the land by rivers. Most has rained down slowly from the surface waters. It contains the remains of countless millions of tiny plants and animals, such as those shown below.

GREENLAND
NORTH AMERICA
EUROPE
AFRICA
SOUTH AMERICA

■ Clay

■ Globigerina ooze ■ Radiolarian ooze □ Pteropod ooze ■ Diatom ooze

Globigerina *Radiolarian* *Pteropod* *Diatoms*

The Pacific Ocean

THE PACIFIC OCEAN is the biggest ocean – by a very long way. It is twice as large as its closest rival, the Atlantic, and covers a third of the Earth's surface.

It stretches from the Arctic in the north to the Antarctic in the south, and from the Americas to Australia and Asia. At its widest point, the Pacific Ocean measures about 11,000 miles (17,700 km) and reaches almost halfway around the Earth. The Pacific is also the deepest of the oceans. On average, its water is 13,800 ft (4,200 m) deep. But it drops to 35,827 ft (10,920 m) in the Mariana Trench. This is the deepest part of the ocean and the deepest point on Earth.

The first people to explore the Pacific were the Polynesians, some 2,000 years ago. They used stick maps, the stars, and cloud formations to find their way. Today, the Pacific is of particular interest to oceanographers because it contains many different seafloor features. These include trenches, mountain ridges, and thousands of volcanic and coral islands.

THE EAST PACIFIC RISE

The East Pacific Rise is an underwater mountain range that runs from north to south down the Pacific Ocean. It marks the boundary of the Pacific crustal plate and the Nazca crustal plate. The East Pacific Rise is a spreading ridge, where volcanic eruptions are constantly pushing the existing seafloor apart and creating areas of new ocean crust. As a result, the floor of the Pacific is getting 4–6 in (12–16 cm) wider each year. The East Pacific Rise is 6,561–9,842 ft (2–3,000 m) high and up to 2.5 miles (4 km) wide. It lies about 10,800 ft (3,300 m) underwater.

Section of the East Pacific Rise at the line A–B above. The vertical scale (height of the section) has been exaggerated to make the features clearer.

Fracture zones

There are long, narrow cracks in the Pacific seafloor, particularly around the East Pacific Rise. These are called fracture zones. The zones stretch from east to west, at right angles to the spreading ridges.

The San Andreas Fault

The San Andreas Fault in the U.S. lies on the border between the Pacific Plate and the North American Plate. It stretches for 270 miles (435 km) across California. This area suffers terrible earthquakes, caused by the two plates slipping and sliding past each other.

NORTH AMERICA
SOUTH
ASIA
INDONESIA
NEW GUINEA
JAPAN
PHILIPPINES
PHILIPPINE TRENCH
JAPAN TRENCH
KURIL TRENCH
MARIANA TRENCH
ALEUTIAN BASIN
Aleutian Islands
ALEUTIAN TRENCH
GULF OF ALASKA SEAMOUNT PROVINCE
EMPEROR SEAMOUNTS
HAWAIIAN RIDGE
Hawaiian Islands
MENDOCINO FRACTURE ZONE
MURRAY FRACTURE ZONE
MOLOKAI FRACTURE ZONE
CLARION FRACTURE ZONE
CLIPPERTON FRACTURE ZONE
GALAPAGOS FRACTURE ZONE
MIDDLE AMERICA TRENCH
San Andreas Fault
SAN ANDREAS FAULT
Galapagos Islands
PERU
Line Islands
CENTRAL PACIFIC BASIN
LINE OF CROSS-SECTION
NORTHWEST PACIFIC BASIN
Marshall Islands
Gilbert Islands
Caroline Islands
Solomon Islands
Tuvalu
Samoa
Marquesas Islands
Tuamotu Archipelago

NORTH AMERICAN PLATE
SOUTH AMERICAN PLATE
COCOS PLATE
NAZCA PLATE
PACIFIC PLATE
EAST PACIFIC RISE
Direction of moving plate
A
B

Depth
6,561 ft (2,000 m)
13,123 ft (4,000 m)
A
B

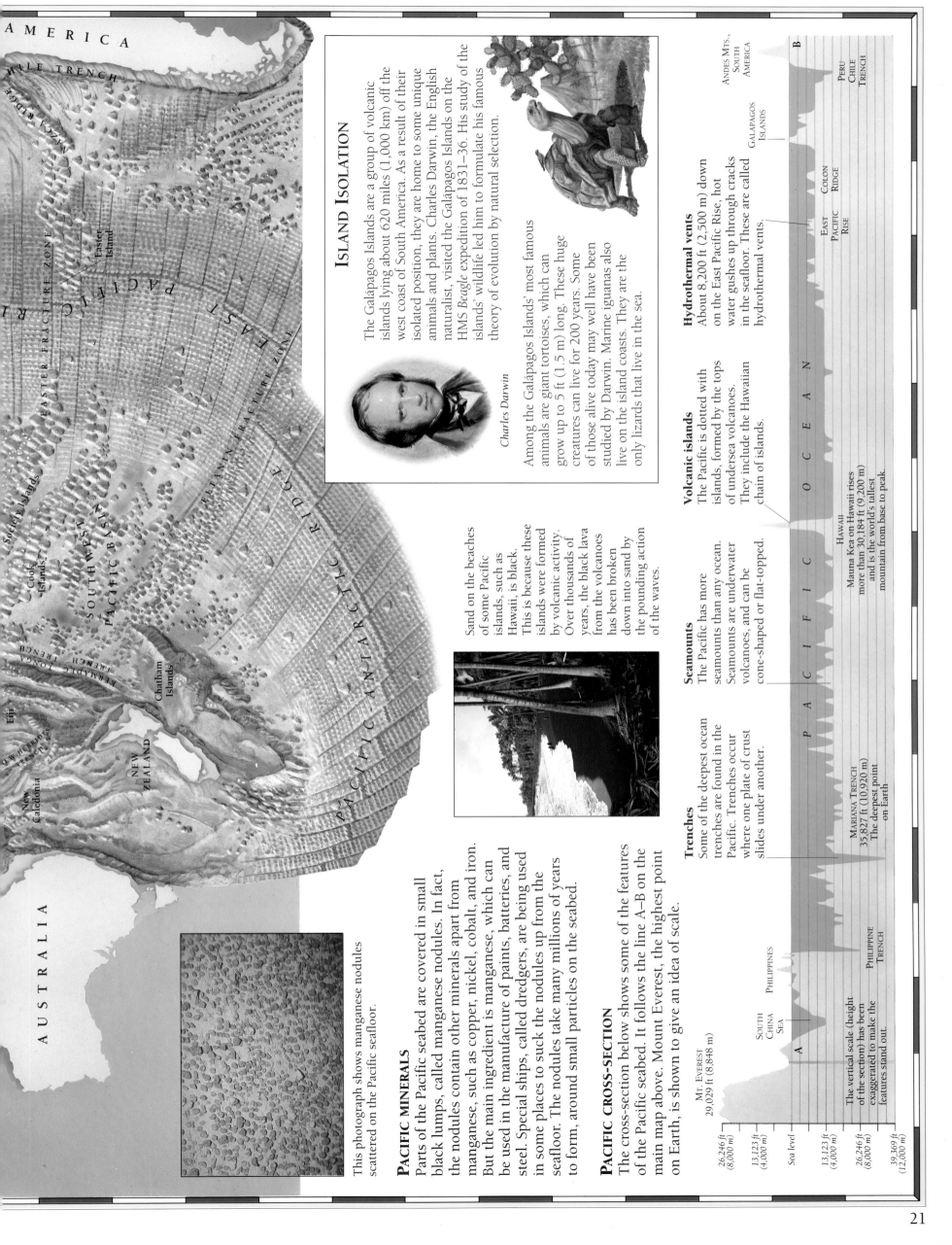

ISLAND ISOLATION

The Galápagos Islands are a group of volcanic islands lying about 620 miles (1,000 km) off the west coast of South America. As a result of their isolated position, they are home to some unique animals and plants. Charles Darwin, the English naturalist, visited the Galápagos Islands on the HMS *Beagle* expedition of 1831–36. His study of the islands' wildlife led him to formulate his famous theory of evolution by natural selection.

Charles Darwin

Among the Galápagos Islands' most famous animals are giant tortoises, which can grow up to 5 ft (1.5 m) long. These huge creatures can live for 200 years. Some of those alive today may well have been studied by Darwin. Marine iguanas also live on the island coasts. They are the only lizards that live in the sea.

Hydrothermal vents
About 8,200 ft (2,500 m) down on the East Pacific Rise, hot water gushes up through cracks in the seafloor. These are called hydrothermal vents.

Volcanic islands
The Pacific is dotted with islands, formed by the tops of undersea volcanoes. They include the Hawaiian chain of islands.

Seamounts
The Pacific has more seamounts than any ocean. Seamounts are underwater volcanoes, and can be cone-shaped or flat-topped.

Trenches
Some of the deepest ocean trenches are found in the Pacific. Trenches occur where one plate of crust slides under another.

This photograph shows manganese nodules scattered on the Pacific seafloor.

PACIFIC MINERALS
Parts of the Pacific seabed are covered in small black lumps, called manganese nodules. In fact, the nodules contain other minerals apart from manganese, such as copper, nickel, cobalt, and iron. But the main ingredient is manganese, which can be used in the manufacture of paints, batteries, and steel. Special ships, called dredgers, are being used in some places to suck the nodules up from the seafloor. The nodules take many millions of years to form, around small particles on the seabed.

PACIFIC CROSS-SECTION
The cross-section below shows some of the features of the Pacific seabed. It follows the line A–B on the main map above. Mount Everest, the highest point on Earth, is shown to give an idea of scale.

The vertical scale (height of the section) has been exaggerated to make the features stand out.

MT. EVEREST 29,029 ft (8,848 m)

MARIANA TRENCH 35,827 ft (10,920 m) The deepest point on Earth

HAWAII Mauna Kea on Hawaii rises more than 30,184 ft (9,200 m) and is the world's tallest mountain from base to peak.

Volcanic Islands

VOLCANOES OCCUR where hot, molten rock, called magma, from deep inside the Earth rises up through cracks or holes in the Earth's crust and solidifies. Thousands of volcanoes grow from the seafloor, many stretching to vast heights that would dwarf even the largest volcanoes on land. In some places, volcanoes grow so tall that their tops break the surface of the sea and form islands. The Hawaiian Islands, shown in the main illustration, are the tops of enormous volcanoes that have grown higher through millions of years of lava eruptions.

It has only recently been possible for scientists to study and map underwater volcanoes, thanks to great advances in technology. They now use instruments such as acoustic mapping systems, powerful cameras, deep-diving research submersibles, and ROVs (remote-operated vehicles).

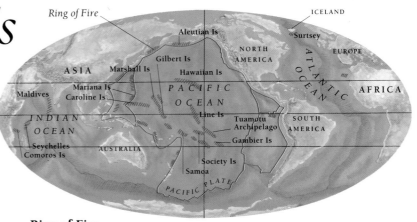

Ring of Fire
The map above shows the position of the world's volcanic islands. Most of these are found in the so-called "Ring of Fire" that circles the edge of the Pacific Plate. Devastating earthquakes, as well as frequent volcanic eruptions, give this ring its name. Chains of islands in the middle of the ring were formed over hot spots (see right).

Older and smaller
Samples taken from lava flows along the Hawaiian island chain show that the islands in the northwest are older than those in the southeast. Samples from Kauai are about five million years old; those from Hawaii are less than a million years old. This is evidence that the Pacific Plate moves like a giant conveyor belt over the fixed hot spot. Erosion has worn away the tops and sides of the oldest, inactive volcanoes.

THREE TYPES OF VOLCANO
Volcanic islands form in one of three ways. Curving arcs of islands are created where one crustal plate slides under another in the subduction process. "Hot spot" volcanoes form over a column of magma rising like a fountain beneath the crust. Volcanic islands can also form along mid-ocean ridges, where two plates of crust move apart and magma oozes up to fill the gap. This process is known as seafloor spreading.

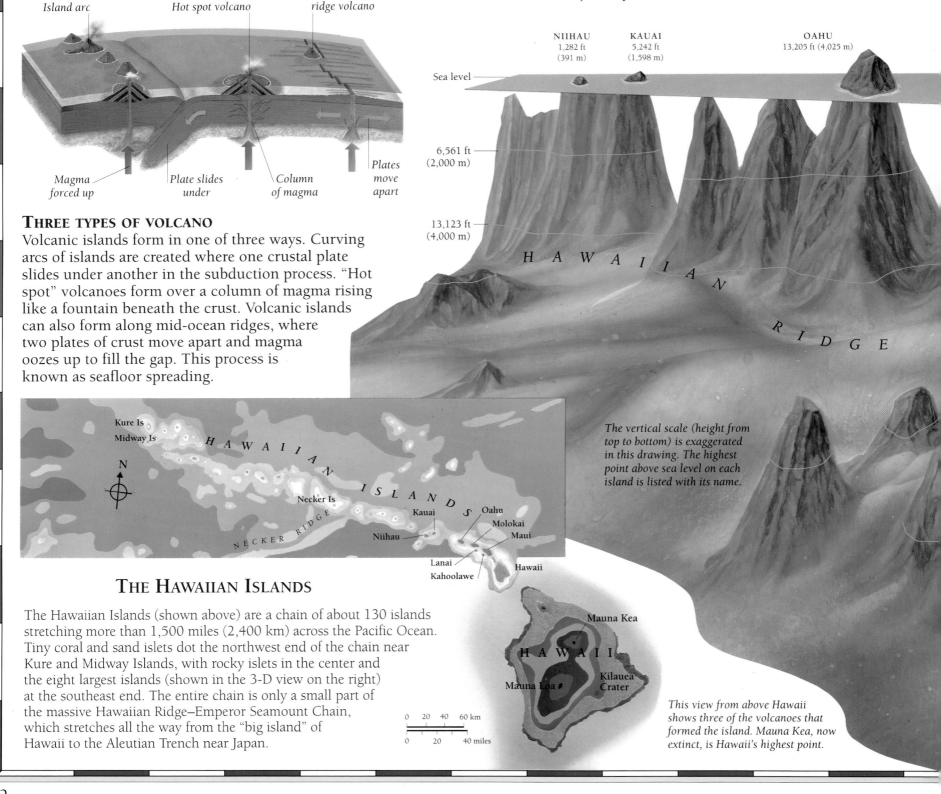

The vertical scale (height from top to bottom) is exaggerated in this drawing. The highest point above sea level on each island is listed with its name.

THE HAWAIIAN ISLANDS

The Hawaiian Islands (shown above) are a chain of about 130 islands stretching more than 1,500 miles (2,400 km) across the Pacific Ocean. Tiny coral and sand islets dot the northwest end of the chain near Kure and Midway Islands, with rocky islets in the center and the eight largest islands (shown in the 3-D view on the right) at the southeast end. The entire chain is only a small part of the massive Hawaiian Ridge–Emperor Seamount Chain, which stretches all the way from the "big island" of Hawaii to the Aleutian Trench near Japan.

This view from above Hawaii shows three of the volcanoes that formed the island. Mauna Kea, now extinct, is Hawaii's highest point.

HOT SPOT VOLCANOES

Thousands of volcanic islands have formed over so-called hot spots in the oceans. These are isolated areas of volcanic activity where plumes of magma rise up through the seafloor. As a plate of the Earth's crust moves across a hot spot, a volcano erupts and a new island is born. The Hawaiian Islands are examples of hot spot volcanoes. Some hot spots have been creating volcanoes for more than 70 million years.

Active volcano

Direction of plate movement

Extinct volcano

1 *Volcano erupts over stationary hot spot, forming a new island.*

2 *Plate carries active volcanoes away, and they no longer erupt.*

3 *The chain of extinct volcanoes grows as the plate moves.*

Hot spot

A volcano on the island of Hawaii sprays molten lava during an eruption. Hawaii was formed by five volcanoes. Two of these, Kilauea and Mauna Loa, are still among the most active volcanoes in the world, erupting every two to three years.

AN ISLAND IS BORN

In 1963, a new volcanic island was created off the south coast of Iceland. It was named Surtsey after an ancient Icelandic god of fire. The island grew quickly. Within four days, it was more than 1,970 ft (600 m) long and 197 ft (60 m) high. Eighteen months later, green plants were found growing on it, and by 1968 Surtsey was home to 40 species of insects and birds. The island stopped erupting in 1967.

Steam and smoke billow from Surtsey as it emerges from the sea off Iceland.

MOLOKAI
4,970 ft (1,515 m)

KAHOOLAWE
1,476 ft (450 m)

LANAI
3,369 ft (1,027 m)

MAUI
10,022 ft (3,055 m)

HAWAII
13,795 ft (4,205 m)

Loihi
Loihi is an active volcano in the Hawaiian chain. Its summit is now 2,950 ft (900 m) below sea level. Scientists think it will break the surface in 10,000–100,000 years' time.

Loihi seamount

Hawaiian hot spot
No one knows the exact size of the hot spot under the island of Hawaii, although it must be large enough to supply the active volcanoes along the chain. Some scientists estimate that the pool of magma is nearly 200 miles (322 km) across. Narrow tunnels feed the magma to each of the volcanoes.

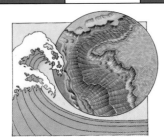

Seamounts

TOWERING ABOVE the ocean floor are huge submerged mountains known as seamounts. Their peaks rise more than 3,280 ft (1,000 m) above the seabed but do not break the surface of the sea. Most seamounts are cone shaped, often with steeply sloping sides. Those with pointed summits are known as sea peaks. Those with flattened summits are called guyots. Although many seamounts appear to rise randomly from the ocean floor, most are found in groups or linear chains, such as the Emperor Seamount Chain shown on these pages. The largest single seamount is the Great Meteor Tablemount in the northeast Atlantic Ocean. It is 13,123 ft (4,000 m) high and more than 62 miles (100 km) wide at its base. Most types of seamounts are formed in the same way as volcanic islands, to which they are related (see previous pages).

THE EMPEROR SEAMOUNTS

Stretching northward in a vast arc across the Pacific Ocean, the Emperor Seamount Chain is one of the longest seamount ranges. The chain begins at the western tip of the Hawaiian Islands and disappears near the Aleutian Trench, nearly 3,700 miles (6,000 km) away. Scientists believe that it is a continuation of the Hawaiian chain. This is because the age of each island and seamount increases as the chain stretches northward, indicating that the entire chain formed over the same hot spot.

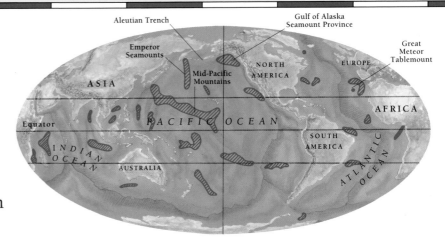

Where seamounts are found
There are hundreds of seamounts in all of the oceans, although they are most plentiful in the Pacific Ocean. The shaded areas on the map above show where groups of seamounts are found. Scientists estimate that there are more than 10,000 seamounts and guyots. The actual number may be twice as high as this. Because seamounts are similar to volcanic islands, they are found in areas where underwater volcanic activity is common.

Age of the seamounts
The seamount closest to the Aleutian end of the chain (number one on the view below) is millions of years older than the seamount that is closest to Hawaii (number eight). The numbers correspond to those on the smaller map (below left).

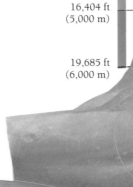

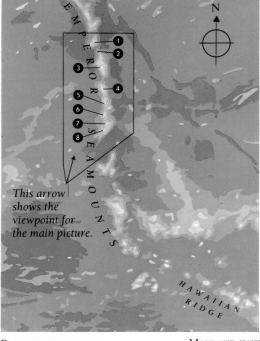

This arrow shows the viewpoint for the main picture.

EMPEROR SEAMOUNTS   MAUI AND HAWAII

Sea surface

Comparative profiles of seamounts (left) and islands

Seamounts rise abruptly from the seafloor, indicating that their bases may be buried by sediment.

Looking from above and underneath the sea
The part of the Emperor Seamount Chain in the box on the small map (left) is shown in the big picture, on the right. The height has been exaggerated to show how sharply the seamounts rise from the flat seafloor. The diagram on the lower left shows the difference in profile between the Emperor Seamounts and two of the biggest Hawaiian islands. Over millions of years, the two volcanic islands of Hawaii and Maui may erode and sink below the surface of the sea to become submerged like the seamounts.

GUYOTS

Guyots are the sunken remains of ancient islands, whose tops have been flattened by the erosive action of the waves. They are particularly common in the North Pacific, where they often form large clusters. At some time in the past, these seamounts were close to the surface of the sea. They sank as the seafloor beneath them subsided. Most are now some 3,280–6,561 ft (1,000–2,000 m) below the surface. Guyots were named after the eighteenth-century Swiss geologist Arnold Guyot.

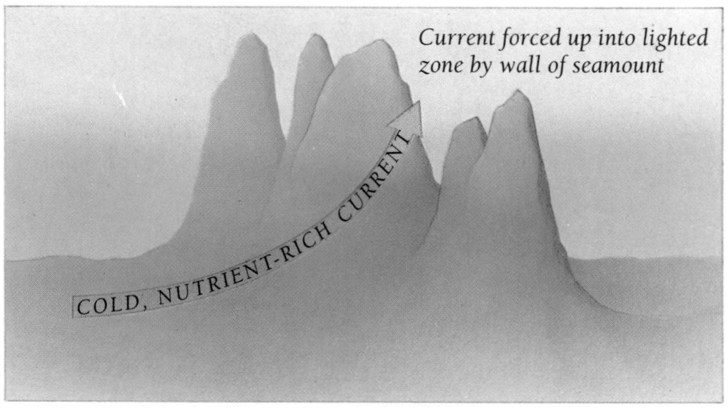

Current forced up into lighted zone by wall of seamount

COLD, NUTRIENT-RICH CURRENT

The diagram on the left shows what happens when deep-sea currents meet the submerged walls of a seamount. The current surges over the walls, or collects in eddies behind them.

Nutrient-rich waters attract feeding fish. Small fish often live in groups, because it is more difficult for a predator to catch a single fish in a large group.

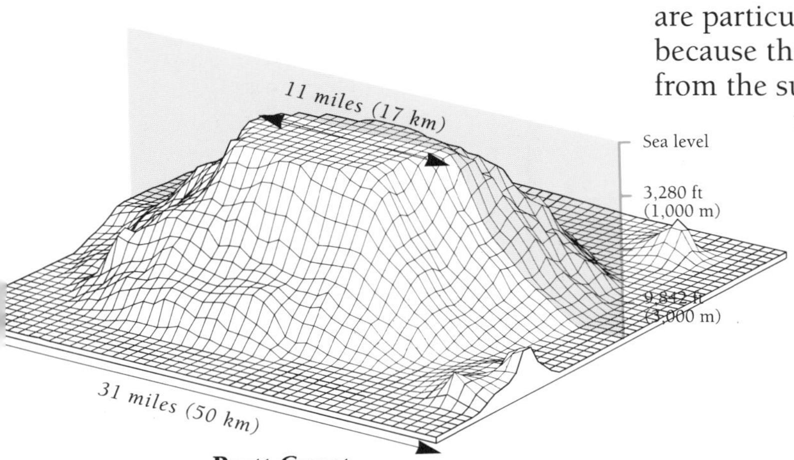

TEEMING WITH LIFE

By comparison with the surrounding deep-sea floor, the upper parts of seamounts and guyots are particularly rich in marine life. This is partly because they are shallower and receive more food from the surface waters. But it is also because, due to their height, seamounts can change the flow of deep-ocean currents. The seamount may lie in the path of a current, forcing the cold, nutrient-rich waters to flow over and around the seamount. Many marine animals take advantage of the food surge and make seamounts their feeding places. Other nutrient-rich currents collect in eddies in the lee of (behind) seamounts.

11 miles (17 km)

Sea level

3,280 ft (1,000 m)

9,842 ft (3,000 m)

31 miles (50 km)

Pratt Guyot

The gigantic Pratt Guyot rises nearly 8,858 ft (2,700 m) from the floor of the Gulf of Alaska, in the northern Pacific Ocean. This computer-created image shows its size and shape.

❻

❼

❽

Black coral

Black coral

Antipatharians, or black corals, are related to reef-building corals. Instead of stony skeletons, however, they have skeletons of black horny material. Like most corals, they are made up of many small individuals called polyps.

Gorgonian coral

FILTER FEEDERS

The currents swirling around a seamount encourage filter-feeding animals, such as the corals and sponges shown below. These creatures attach themselves to the sides of the seamount and sift food particles from the water flowing past. The currents also carry nutrients. These help phytoplankton to grow which, in turn, provide food for tiny sea animals and larger fish.

Gorgonian growth

Gorgonians, or horny corals, are sometimes found 500 ft (150 m) down on the sides of seamounts. They often grow into large fan shapes spread out across the currents. This gives these filter-feeding animals the best access to food particles in the water. The discovery of huge populations of gorgonians on several seamounts in the Emperor Chain in the 1970s caused a crash in the price of precious corals on the world market.

Sponges

Sponges attach themselves to the sides of seamounts. The outsides of their bodies are covered with many small holes called pores. Sponges take in water through these pores and filter it for food. They expel the filtered water and wastes through one or a few larger holes.

Deep-Sea Trenches

DEEP-SEA TRENCHES are the deepest parts of the seabed, and the deepest points on planet Earth. They occur at the edges of two oceanic plates, or of an oceanic and a continental plate, where one plate melts back into the Earth by a process called subduction. Subduction balances out the effects of seafloor spreading (see page 37). Without it, the Earth would have increased its size by half in the last 200 million years.

The trenches are long, narrow, V-shaped seabed valleys. Some plunge to depths of 26,246–32,808 ft (8,000–10,000 m). Even 50 years ago no one imagined the oceans could reach such depths. The trenches lie 6,561–13,123 ft (2,000–4,000 m) below the rest of the seafloor. They are pitch black and freezing cold, with massive underwater pressures. Underwater earthquakes (seaquakes) and volcanic eruptions are common in deep-sea trenches because of the moving crust.

HOW TRENCHES ARE FORMED

Deep-sea trenches form when the Earth's crustal plates collide, and one is forced beneath the other. This is called subduction. When an oceanic plate collides with a continental plate, the seabed is subducted under the land. This forms a trench and also pushes up a range of volcanic mountains on land. When two oceanic plates collide, the subducted plate melts back into the Earth.

Challenger Deep in the Mariana Trench is the deepest point on Earth.

The Aleutian Trench is the longest trench on Earth.

Where trenches are found
The majority of trenches are found at the boundaries of the plates which form the Pacific Ocean seafloor. There are some smaller trenches in the Atlantic and Indian Oceans. The map above shows both the positions of the two trenches featured on these pages – the Peru-Chile Trench and the Mariana Trench – as well as the edges of their adjacent crustal plates.

LIFE IN THE HADAL ZONE
Oceanographers divide life in the sea into zones, by depth. The deep-sea trenches form the hadal zone, the deepest habitat of all. At a depth of more than 19,685 ft (6,000 m) below the surface, the amazing animals of the hadal zone have to cope with crushing pressure, darkness, and freezing water. They include sea cucumbers, anemones, crustaceans, polychaete worms, and some mollusks.

This photograph of some of the unusual creatures that live around a hydrothermal vent was taken from the submersible *Alvin* (part of which can be seen) in an area near the Mariana Trench.

Sea anemone

Sea cucumber

Polychaete worm

CONTINENTAL PLATE

Lithosphere (crust and upper mantle)

Subduction of oceanic plate

Andes Mts., Chile

Continental crust

Peru-Chile Trench

Oceanic crust

Lithosphere

OCEANIC PLATE

Ocean and continent collide
The Andes Mountains were pushed up about 80 million years ago by subduction along the coast of Chile. The deepest point of the resulting Peru-Chile Trench is 25,050 ft (7,635 m).

OCEANIC PLATE

Island arc

Guam

Mariana Trench

Direction of subduction

Oceanic crust

Lithosphere

OCEANIC PLATE

Oceanic plates collide
The Mariana Trench in the Pacific (shown in this diagram) formed when two oceanic plates collided. The subduction process also pushed up an arc of volcanic islands, including the island of Guam.

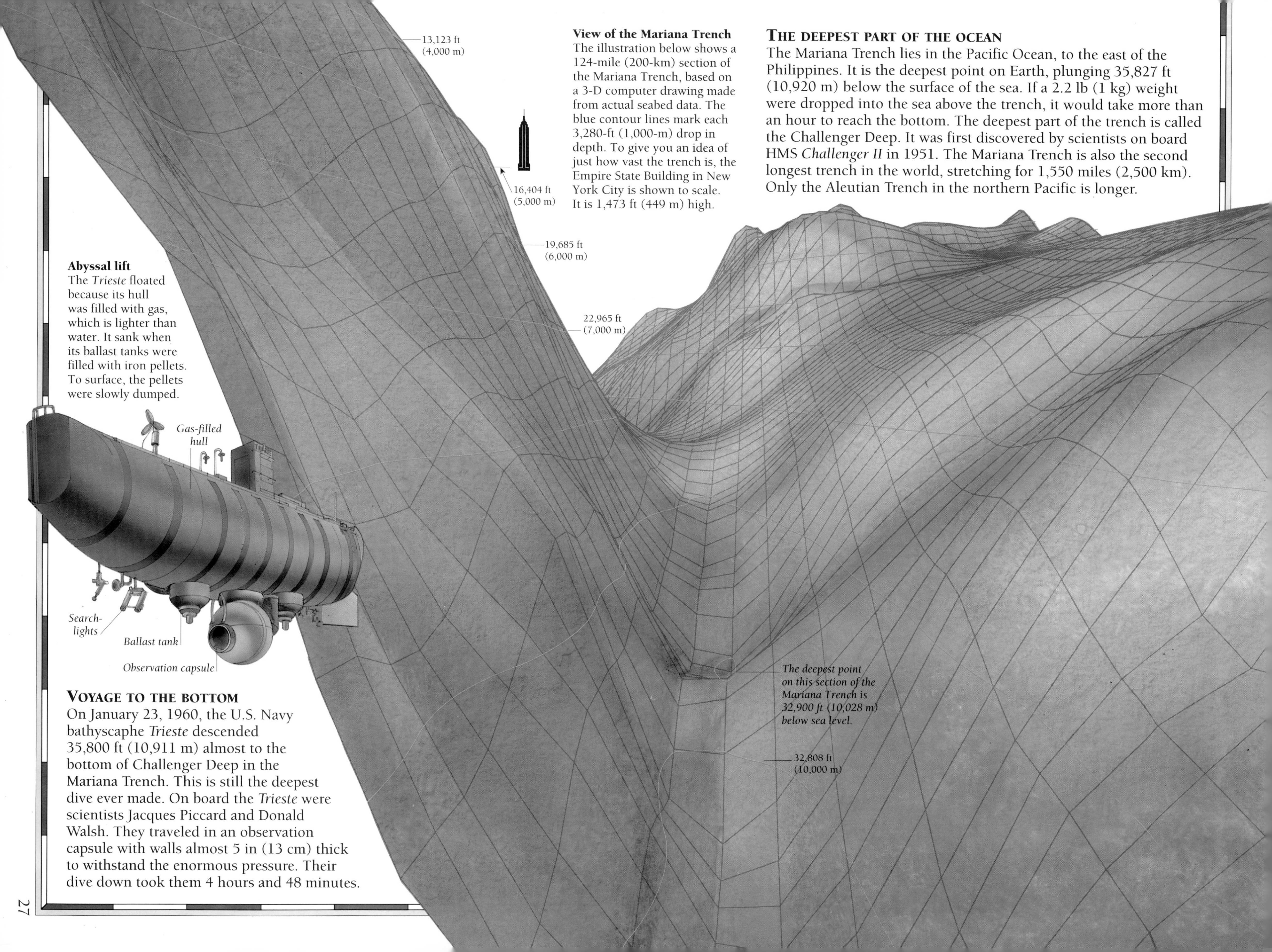

THE DEEPEST PART OF THE OCEAN

The Mariana Trench lies in the Pacific Ocean, to the east of the Philippines. It is the deepest point on Earth, plunging 35,827 ft (10,920 m) below the surface of the sea. If a 2.2 lb (1 kg) weight were dropped into the sea above the trench, it would take more than an hour to reach the bottom. The deepest part of the trench is called the Challenger Deep. It was first discovered by scientists on board HMS *Challenger II* in 1951. The Mariana Trench is also the second longest trench in the world, stretching for 1,550 miles (2,500 km). Only the Aleutian Trench in the northern Pacific is longer.

View of the Mariana Trench

The illustration below shows a 124-mile (200-km) section of the Mariana Trench, based on a 3-D computer drawing made from actual seabed data. The blue contour lines mark each 3,280-ft (1,000-m) drop in depth. To give you an idea of just how vast the trench is, the Empire State Building in New York City is shown to scale. It is 1,473 ft (449 m) high.

13,123 ft (4,000 m)

16,404 ft (5,000 m)

19,685 ft (6,000 m)

22,965 ft (7,000 m)

The deepest point on this section of the Mariana Trench is 32,900 ft (10,028 m) below sea level.

32,808 ft (10,000 m)

Abyssal lift

The *Trieste* floated because its hull was filled with gas, which is lighter than water. It sank when its ballast tanks were filled with iron pellets. To surface, the pellets were slowly dumped.

Gas-filled hull

Search-lights

Ballast tank

Observation capsule

VOYAGE TO THE BOTTOM

On January 23, 1960, the U.S. Navy bathyscaphe *Trieste* descended 35,800 ft (10,911 m) almost to the bottom of Challenger Deep in the Mariana Trench. This is still the deepest dive ever made. On board the *Trieste* were scientists Jacques Piccard and Donald Walsh. They traveled in an observation capsule with walls almost 5 in (13 cm) thick to withstand the enormous pressure. Their dive down took them 4 hours and 48 minutes.

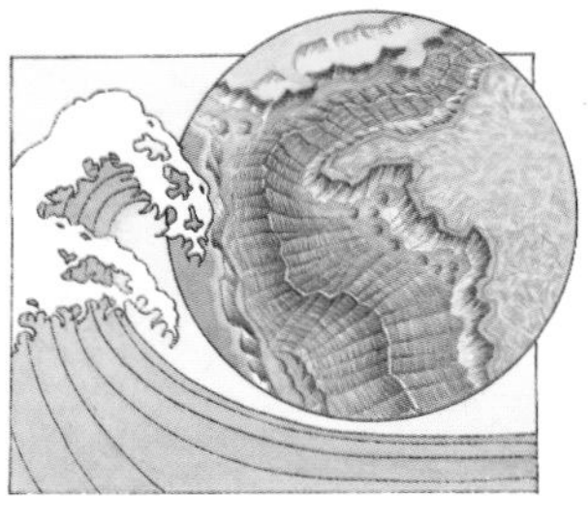

Black Smokers

SCIENTISTS INVESTIGATING volcanoes deep under the Pacific Ocean made a remarkable discovery in 1977. Hot, mineral-rich water shooting up from cracks in the seabed provides a home for huge colonies of extraordinary animals. Many of these had never been seen before. At 8,200 ft (2,500 m) below the surface, the deep sea is usually dark, deserted, and very cold. The water around these cracks, or hydrothermal vents, however, can reach temperatures of over 572°F (300°C). Sulfur, dissolved in the water, is heated by rocks in the crust below, and gushes up. This mixture is poisonous to most creatures, yet it is the only reason vent animals can survive. Clumps of bacteria use it for nourishment and they, in turn, provide food for the other creatures.

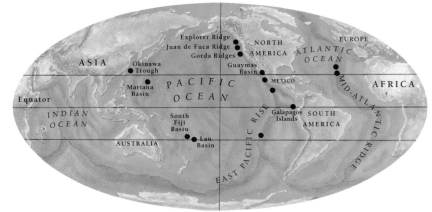

Where vents are found

Hydrothermal vents are mainly found along spreading seabed ridges. Vent sites in the Pacific Ocean include areas around the Galápagos Islands and the East Pacific Rise off Mexico. Other sites lie on the Mid-Atlantic Ridge and in the northwest Pacific Ocean.

TUBE WORM GIANTS

The most amazing members of the vent community are the giant tube worms, *Riftia*. They grow in great clusters around the vents. They have neither mouths nor digestive organs, so they cannot feed on any rare fragments of food falling from the surface. Instead, they rely on thick colonies of bacteria living inside their bodies. The worms supply hydrogen sulfide, which they extract from the sulfur-rich water around them. The bacteria use the hydrogen sulfide to make food for themselves and the worms.

A tube worm can be more than 10 ft (3 m) long – much longer than a person.

Tube worms at the Galápagos vent site, photographed from a submersible. The object on the left is a probe to measure the temperature of the gushing hot water.

The ends of the worms protrude from their tubes.

White crabs

Crazy chimneys

As the hot water shoots up, it deposits sulfur and other minerals on the sides of the vents. This builds chimneys up to 33 ft (10 m) tall. The sulfur also colors the water black, earning the vents the name "black smokers." The amount and variety of life discovered here astonished scientists. The discovery of chemosynthesis (see below) was also astonishing – it meant that biology textbooks had to be rewritten around the world.

DISCOVERING THE VENT SITES

The first hydrothermal vent sites were found about 200 miles (320 km) northeast of the Galápagos Islands off the west coast of Ecuador, in South America. They were explored by three scientists on board the submersible, *Alvin*, which is operated by Woods Hole Oceanographic Institute in Massachusetts, U.S. More vents were later discovered on the Colon Ridge northwest of the Galápagos Islands, and at sites on the East Pacific Rise and the Mid-Atlantic Ridge in 1985.

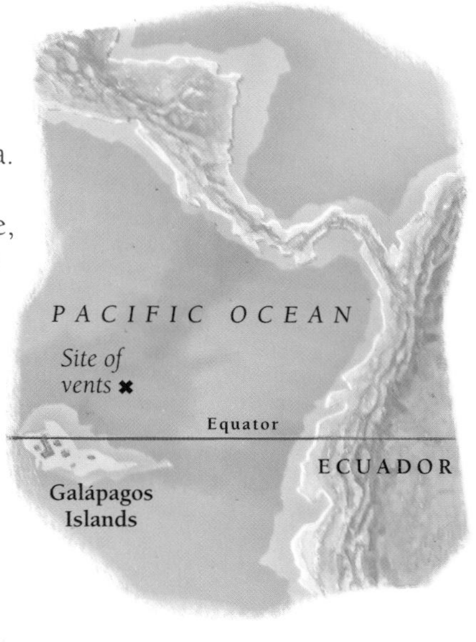

PACIFIC OCEAN

Site of vents ✖

Equator

ECUADOR

Galápagos Islands

FOOD CHEMISTRY

Where there is light, plants make their food by a process called photosynthesis. The green pigment chlorophyll in their leaves uses sunlight to make a simple food. But no sunlight reaches the deep ocean. Instead, the bacteria use sulfur in the water to make food. This process is called chemosynthesis.

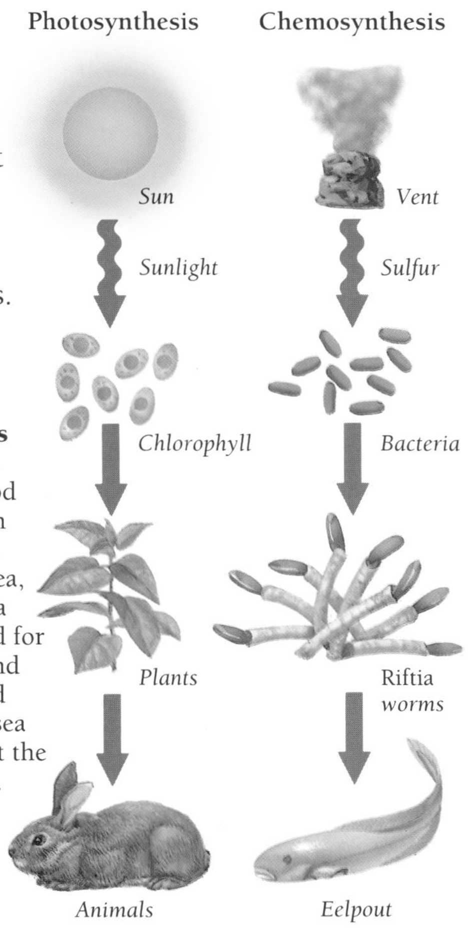

Photosynthesis Chemosynthesis

Sun Vent

Sunlight Sulfur

Chlorophyll Bacteria

Plants *Riftia worms*

Animals Eelpout

Food chains

Chlorophyll provides food for plants on land (right). Under the sea, vent bacteria provide food for the *Riftia*, and eelpouts and other deep-sea creatures eat the tube worms.

Current crustaceans

Vent crustaceans include squat lobsters and crabs who are completely blind, with no eyes in their eye sockets. Both scavenge for scraps of food in the currents stirred up by the gushing hot vent water.

Underwater dandelions

At the vent sites, scientists discovered an odd creature called a siphonophore. It looks like a dandelion, but is in fact related to the jellyfish. It hangs just above the seabed, held in place by fine, thread-like tentacles.

Giant clams

Clams and mussels

Giants of the vent community include mussels and clams that grow to be as much as a foot (30 cm) long. Like the tube worms, they rely on bacteria inside their bodies for food.

Something fishy

Very few fish have been found near vents. However, 10-in (25-cm)-long fish called eelpouts have been seen nibbling at the tube worms and investigating the clams.

Squat lobster

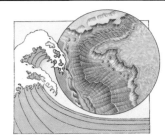

Coral Reefs

CORAL REEFS ARE often described as underwater tropical rain forests or gardens. Like the rain forests, they are full of color and life. They swarm with brilliantly colored fish, starfish, giant clams, and sea slugs. In fact, nearly one-third of all the world's species of fish live in coral reefs. Coral reefs can cover vast areas – often thousands of square miles (kilometers) – yet they are built by tiny creatures called polyps. Most polyps grow in partnership with tiny plants called algae. For that reason, coral can grow only in warm, shallow water where there is plenty of sunlight that the algae need to make food. There have been coral reefs on Earth for more than 450 million years. Coral is formed very slowly. It takes about 20 years for a colony the size of a basketball to build up.

Reefs around the world
There are about 230,000 sq miles (600,000 sq km) of coral reefs in the world. They grow only in shallow seas, in water temperatures of 68°F (18°C) and above. Major reefs are found in the Pacific and Indian oceans.

Lagoon

Coral sand
The white sand commonly found in coral reefs is partly made of ground-up shells and corals. It is also produced by algae growing on the reef.

Sea level
Coral is very sensitive to changes in sea level. It can grow only in shallow water. If the sea level rises too much, it may die.

WHAT IS CORAL?
Coral is formed from the hard outer skeletons of tiny animals called polyps. Until about 200 years ago, people thought that coral polyps were plants. In fact, they are related to sea anemones and jellyfish. Most polyps are only about ¼ in (5 mm) across. Reef-building hard corals live in huge colonies. Soft corals and the closely related gorgonian, or horny, corals do not have stony outer skeletons.

Continuous barrier
Barrier reefs form on the sea-facing side of long, narrow lagoons. They follow the contours of the coastline.

A LIVING STONE
The stony, cuplike casings built by hard coral polyps protect their soft bodies. The cups are made from chemicals that the polyp extracts from seawater. Only the top surface of the reef is alive. The tiny, one-celled algae that live inside the polyps' bodies help them secrete limestone. This cements the reef together.

A polyp expands to catch its food, using the tentacles around its mouth. The tentacles contain stinging cells to stun or kill prey.

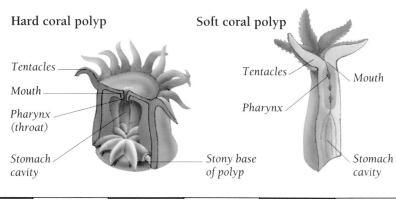

Hard coral polyp

Tentacles
Mouth
Pharynx (throat)
Stomach cavity
Stony base of polyp

Soft coral polyp

Tentacles
Mouth
Pharynx
Stomach cavity

DIFFERENT KINDS OF CORAL REEFS

In 1842, the British naturalist Charles Darwin described the types of coral reefs. His definitions are still used today. There are three main types of reef. Fringing reefs grow in shallow water along the shore on rocky coastlines. Barrier reefs also grow along the shore, but they are separated from it by lagoons (shallow saltwater lakes) or straits. Atoll islands begin as reefs growing on the slopes of volcanoes. The volcanoes then sink, leaving the atoll behind. Atolls surround deeper lagoons.

Seaward edge

On the reef's seaward edge, the waves throw up debris, which forms ridges full of pools and holes. These are home to thousands of fish.

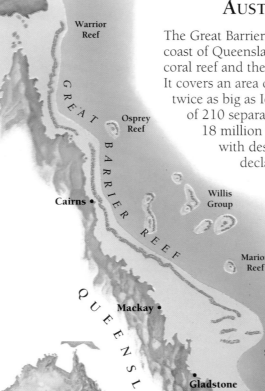

AUSTRALIA'S GREAT BARRIER REEF

The Great Barrier Reef stretches for 1,260 miles (2,028 km) off the coast of Queensland in northeastern Australia. It is the world's largest coral reef and the biggest structure ever made by living things. It covers an area of more than 80,000 sq miles (207,000 sq km) – twice as big as Iceland. The reef is not a single barrier, but consists of 210 separate reefs. The Great Barrier Reef began to grow about 18 million years ago. Recently, the reef has been threatened with destruction by tourism and pollution. In 1983, it was declared a marine park. Special zones are set aside for recreation, fishing, and snorkeling.

The Dingo Reef complex is situated in the south-central part of the Great Barrier Reef.

FANTASTIC FORMATIONS

Corals grow in an amazing variety of beautiful shapes and patterns. Some look like miniature trees. Others resemble mushrooms, dinner plates, or feathers. Reef-building coral grows in layers. The way a coral grows depends on its species, how it copes with the battering of waves, and how much it has to compete with its neighbors for space and sunlight. The color of coral is only "skin-deep." It is produced by the top, living layer of coral. The dead coral beneath is white.

Gorgonian fan coral

Orange-yellow fan coral often grows in deeper water in the Atlantic and Pacific oceans.

Gorgonian coral

This coral has a flexible, horny skeleton, not a rigid casing. It often grows in thickets under ledges or on the roofs of caves in the reef.

Staghorn coral

This hardy branching coral can grow again from just a tiny broken piece. Its branches allow it to grow upward toward the sunlight.

Brain coral

Brain coral gets its name because it looks like a human brain. Its polyps grow in ridges. This coral can grow to more than 6 ft 6 in (2 m) across.

Daisy coral

Many corals look like exotic flowers. Daisy corals are hard corals with brilliant colors.

How branching coral grows

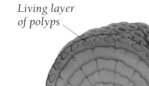

Living polyps at ends of branches

Polyp divides to form branch

Original polyp

How mound coral grows

Living layer of polyps

Original polyp

Marine Life of Reefs

CORAL REEFS TEEM with wildlife. Every nook and cranny is used as a hiding place or shelter. Fish dart among the branches of coral and hide in small caves. Predators, such as moray eels, lurk in larger caves, on the lookout for passing prey.

The reefs are successful habitats because every available source of nourishment is used and recycled through a series of food chains. Each chain begins with microscopic plants called algae. Some float free in the water, while others live in the bodies of the corals. Fish and starfish graze on the coral itself. In turn, these creatures are preyed on by reef hunters, such as barracudas and sharks.

A coral reef is a finely balanced habitat, and a fragile one. All over the world, reefs are under threat from divers, shell and coral collectors, companies exploring for oil and other minerals, and from pollution.

CREATURES OF THE CORAL REEF

The warm, sunny waters of a reef are home to a huge variety of creatures, who present a dazzling display of colors, shapes, and sizes. The richest reefs contain thousands of species of fish and coral, together with starfish, giant clams, and sea slugs. In the densely packed reef, the brilliant colors of creatures such as the butterfly fish act as identity tags. They enable the fish to recognize their own species among the crowd.

Lionfish (below)
The lionfish's bright colors act as a warning. Hidden behind its fins, the fish has spines that can inject a deadly poison into an attacker.

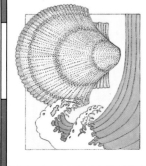

Reef shark
Sleek reef sharks patrol the reef edge after dark. They can sense the movements made by sick or injured fish and swim straight in for the kill.

Sea turtle
At breeding time, female sea turtles leave the water and lay their eggs on the sandy beaches of coral islands. The baby turtles have a dangerous journey to the sea. Many are eaten by crabs and seagulls.

Manta ray
Manta rays swim by flapping their huge wings. Some have wingspans of up to 20 ft (6 m). They sometimes make spectacular leaps out of the water.

Black noddy
These seabirds dip to the surface to feed. They also catch flying fish in midair.

Frigate bird
Frigate birds are pirates, stealing fish from other seabirds. The male has an unusual courtship display. He inflates his bright-red throat pouch like a balloon to attract a mate.

Lion's mane jellyfish
The lion's mane jellyfish gets its name from its thick manelike mass of tentacles and its tawny color. The stinging tentacles may be up to 33 ft (10 m) long.

Coral trout
The coral trout lurks among the coral, looking half asleep. Until, that is, a small fish strays from its school. Then the trout lunges and gobbles it up.

Sea snake (below)
There are about 50 species of sea snake in the tropical oceans. All of them are venomous and use poison to kill their prey. Among their adaptations for life in the sea are flattened tails for swimming.

Barracuda
Barracudas are fierce hunters of the coral reef, often more feared than sharks. They have jaws full of razor-sharp teeth, and powerful streamlined bodies for swimming fast after prey. They often hunt in large schools.

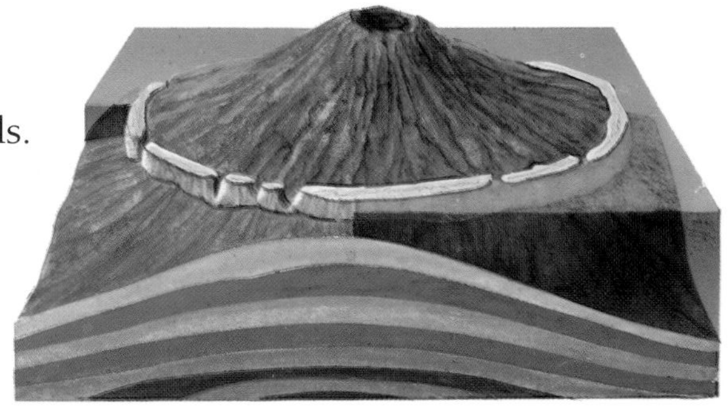

A coral reef grows around the base of an island formed by the top of an underwater volcano.

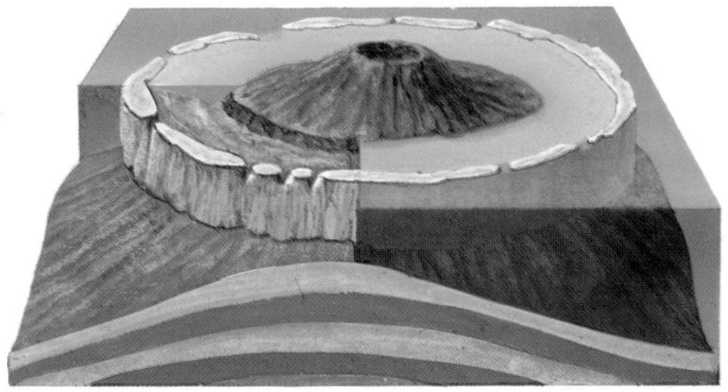

As the sea level rises, or the land sinks, the volcano disappears into the sea. The reef continues to grow at the same rate as before.

The volcanic island is now completely covered in water. The reef remains as a group of small, low-lying islands arranged around a lagoon.

Seen from the air, the atoll of Tahiti looks like a ring of islands. The dormant volcano beneath the surface of the water supports both the reef and the islands.

CORAL ATOLLS

Small circular or horseshoe-shaped groups of coral islands are called atolls. They surround deep lagoons which, together with the coral itself, form habitats rich in marine life. Atolls form from fringing reefs that grow around the cones of underwater volcanoes (right). As the sea level rises, or the volcano sinks into the sea, the reef continues to grow upward to form a ring of islands.

Sea snake

Eagle ray

Blue-ringed octopus (far left)
This octopus is only about 1½ in (3 cm) long but its poison is strong enough to kill a human. It uses it to kill its prey of mollusks and crabs.

Moray eel
The moray eel is one of the reef's top predators. It allows shrimps in its mouth to pick bits of leftover food off its teeth.

Crown-of-thorns starfish
Large chunks of the Great Barrier Reef have been eaten by crown-of-thorns starfish. To feed, a starfish pushes its stomach out through its mouth and slowly digests the polyps. Then it pulls its stomach in again.

Clownfish
Clownfish live among the tentacles of sea anemones. A mucus coating protects the fish from the tentacles' sting.

Nudibranch
Like land slugs, nudibranchs, or sea slugs, have no shell. Their bodies are brilliantly colored.

Sea anemone
Sea anemones extend their stinging tentacles to catch small sea creatures. If danger threatens, they can pull their tentacles in again in a flash.

Baler shell

Brittle star

Feather star
Feather stars anchor themselves on a rock and spread out their arms to strain plankton from the water. These delicate animals are related to starfish.

Sea urchin
Sea urchins have hard shells covered with sharp spines. They graze on algae and tiny creatures that live on the rocks, grinding away at them with their hard teeth.

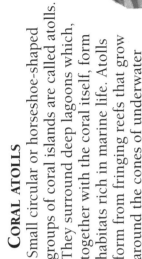

The Story of the Coelacanth

Fossil evidence convinced many scientists that a fish called the coelacanth became extinct about 60 million years ago. In 1938, however, they were amazed when South African fishermen caught a living coelacanth in the Indian Ocean. In fact, the fish was well known to people living on the Comoros Islands, who used its rough scales as sandpaper. This bulky, bluish gray fish spends its time drifting just above the ocean floor. Unlike most fish, which lay eggs, the coelacanth gives birth to live young.

The coelacanth is about 6 ft 6 in (2 m) long, and weighs 126 lb (57 kg)

The Indian Ocean

THE INDIAN OCEAN IS THE THIRD largest of the world's oceans. It covers an area of some 28,350,000 sq miles (73,426,000 sq km), about a fifth of the total area covered by the oceans. It has an average depth of 12,762 ft (3,890 m). Its deepest point is at 24,441 ft (7,450 m) in the Java Trench. The Indian Ocean formed about 140 million years ago, when the ancient continent of Gondwanaland (see page 9) began to break up, separating India and Antarctica from Africa.

One of the features that distinguishes the Indian Ocean from the other oceans is the pattern of its currents. In the other oceans, the currents follow the same path all year. In the northern Indian Ocean, however, they change course twice a year. Blown by the monsoon winds, they flow toward Africa in winter, then in the opposite direction toward India in summer. The Indian Ocean is also unique because it contains the saltiest sea (the Red Sea) and the warmest sea (the Persian Gulf) on Earth.

THE RED SEA

The Red Sea is a narrow branch of the Indian Ocean that separates Africa from Arabia. It is about 1,180 miles (1,900 km) long and 186 miles (300 km) across at its widest point – and it is growing wider. This is because it lies on a spreading ridge that has been moving apart for the past 25 million years, pushing Africa and Arabia farther apart. Millions of years from now, the Red Sea could be as wide as today's Atlantic Ocean.

The Ganges and Indus fans

Two of the world's greatest rivers, the Indus and the Ganges, flow into the Indian Ocean. They carry huge amounts of sediment from the land into the sea. Over time, this sediment has built up into vast submarine fans. The Ganges fan is by far the biggest mass of sediment on Earth, stretching across 1,240 miles (2,000 km).

The Java Trench

The only major trench in the Indian Ocean is the Java Trench. Scientists think that it marks the line along which the Australian plate has been subducted under the Eurasian plate.

Krakatoa

In 1883, a series of massive volcanic eruptions around the Java Trench blew away two-thirds of the island of Krakatoa. A gigantic tsunami swept over the islands of Java and Sumatra, killing thousands of people and leaving many more homeless.

SUMATRA

INDONESIA

JAVA TRENCH

Krakatoa

JAVA

B

BAY OF BENGAL

INVESTIGATOR RIDGE

NINETY EAST RIDGE

Brahmaputra

Ganges

GANGES FAN

INDIA

SRI LANKA

MID-INDIAN OCEAN BASIN

Indus

INDUS FAN

CHAGOS-LACCADIVE PLATEAU

Maldives

MID-INDIAN RIDGE

ARABIAN SEA

ARABIAN BASIN

CARLSBERG RIDGE

MASCARENE PLATEAU

Mauritius

Réunion

ARABIA

SOMALI BASIN

Seychelles

RED SEA

Comoros Islands

LINE OF CROSS-SECTION

A

MADAGASCAR

AFRICA

AUSTRALIA

SOUTHEAST INDIAN RIDGE

SOUTHWEST INDIAN RIDGE

KERGUELEN PLATEAU

Kerguelen

AGULHAS BASIN

AGULHAS PLATEAU

Island of Mahé, Seychelles

THE SEABED IN PROFILE

The cross-section on the right follows the line A–B on the map above, from the east coast of Africa to the west coast of Java. The section shows a profile of the major plateaus, ridges, and basins of the Indian Ocean seabed. Its plateaus are unusually shallow. They may be the remains of small microcontinents, stranded and left to subside when the large continents drifted apart.

EXOTIC ISLANDS

The Indian Ocean is littered with clusters of coral islands. Among the best known are the Seychelles and the Maldives. The Maldive Islands lie to the southwest of Sri Lanka and consist of more than a thousand islands, three-quarters of which are uninhabited. The coral reefs that fringe the islands teem with brightly colored clownfish and damselfish, sea anemones, and prowling reef sharks.

THE MID-OCEAN RIDGE SYSTEM

The most striking feature of the Indian Ocean seabed is the huge, upside-down-Y-shaped mid-ocean ridge. One arm of the Y runs around Africa and joins the Mid-Atlantic Ridge. The other runs around the south of Australia to meet the East Pacific Rise. The ridge runs north through the Indian Ocean, then west toward the Red Sea, where it is known as the Carlsberg Ridge.

Mascarene Plateau

The rocks in this plateau point to its origins as a microcontinent. They are not volcanic, like most rocks found in ocean basins. Instead, they are similar to those rocks that form the continents.

Mid-Indian Ocean Basin

The mid-ocean ridges divide the ocean bed into several basins. The remote Mid-Indian Ocean Basin contains smooth, almost level plains. These are among the flattest places on Earth.

Ninety East Ridge

The Ninety East Ridge is some 1,700 miles (2,735 km) long. Deep-sea drilling has shown that the ridge was once close to the surface of the sea but sank as the seafloor spread.

Huge seagrass beds, like these off the west coast of Australia, provide an ample food supply for sea turtles, sea snakes, and dugongs. They also help to protect the coastline from erosion.

Dugong

INDIAN OCEAN LIFE

The warm tropical waters of the Indian Ocean provide the ideal environment for a rich variety of marine life. Some 4,000 species of fish live near the shores, many of these unique to the Indian Ocean. Farther out to sea, the fish include flying fish, sunfish, marlin, and tuna. There are also rich mangrove forests and seagrass beds. Large, rare sea mammals, called dugongs, browse among the seagrass meadows, particularly off the west coast of Australia.

Seabed profile cross-section

A — AFRICA — MOZAMBIQUE CHANNEL — MADAGASCAR — MASCARENE BASIN — MASCARENE PLATEAU — MID-INDIAN RIDGE — MID-INDIAN OCEAN BASIN — NINETY EAST RIDGE — INVESTIGATOR RIDGE — JAVA TRENCH — JAVA — B

INDIAN OCEAN

Sea level

6,561 ft (2,000 m)

13,123 ft (4,000 m)

19,685 ft (6,000 m)

26,246 ft (8,000 m)

Mid-Ocean Ridges

THE LONGEST MOUNTAIN RANGE on Earth is submerged deep beneath the sea. It is formed by the mid-ocean ridges, interconnected chains of mountains that twist and branch through each of the world's oceans. Together, they span a distance of some 4,038 miles (6,500 km). These mountain ranges are formed by lava that oozes up from the seabed, cools, and then hardens. Some break the surface to form islands, such as Iceland. The longest individual ridge is the Mid-Atlantic Ridge. It runs the entire length of the Atlantic Ocean, splitting it in two.

Mid-ocean ridges are centers of seafloor spreading, a process by which new ocean crust is made. Seafloor spreading and subduction (see pages 8-9) are the two forces responsible for changing the size and shape of the oceans – something that is happening all the time. New crust is made at the ridges, and swallowed up (subducted) at the deep-sea trenches.

Where mid-ocean ridges are found
The map below shows the "centers" of the mid-ocean ridges and the areas of fracture zones (see next page) around them. It also shows the location of the three ridge sections featured on these pages – the Carlsberg Ridge in the Indian Ocean, the East Pacific Rise in the Pacific, and the Mid-Atlantic Ridge in the Atlantic.

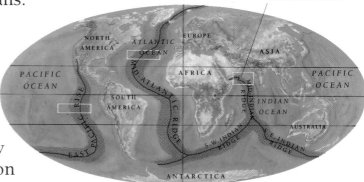

THE CARLSBERG RIDGE
A mid-ocean ridge runs through the Indian Ocean in the shape of a huge, upside-down letter Y. One arm goes around southern Africa and joins the Mid-Atlantic Ridge. The second arm bends around Australia. The central branch forms the Carlsberg Ridge in the northern part of the ocean. This ridge swings west to join up with the Red Sea. The main picture shows this part of the Carlsberg Ridge.

Ocean ridges span huge widths, from 310–3,100 miles (500–5,000 km). All the ridges put together cover about 20 percent of the Earth's surface.

Millions of lumps of pillow lava like the ones above pile up alongside the mid-ocean ridges.

PILLOW LAVA
The rock most commonly found in the crust of the seafloor is a type of lava called basalt. It forms ridges and seamounts and lies underneath the sediment-covered abyssal plains. When basalt erupts underwater and cools quickly, it forms large, round, pillow-shaped lumps, hence its name.

The age of the ocean floor
Although no part of the seafloor is more than 200 million years old, it is youngest at the mid-ocean ridges. The age of the seafloor on either side of the ridge increases as the distance from the ridge increases.

SEAFLOOR SPREADING

At the mid-ocean ridges, hot, molten lava oozes up at the boundary of two plates of crust. The lava cools and solidifies to form new ocean crust. As it does so, it pushes the older crust away to either side of the ridge. This process is known as seafloor spreading. New ocean crust is being made all the time. Over millions of years, it has been layered and pushed up to form the mountains of the mid-ocean ridges. With all this crust being made, you might expect the Earth to get bigger each year. But it does not, because ocean crust is constantly being destroyed at subduction zones, to balance things out.

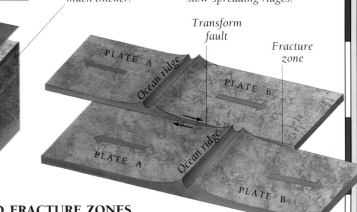

This profile of part of the East Pacific Rise shows the gentle slopes formed by runny lava.

Sea level
6,561 ft (2,000 m)
13,123 ft (4,000 m)

Fast-spreading ridges

Ridges usually spread equally on either side, but some spread more quickly than others. The East Pacific Rise spreads about 5–6 in (12–16 cm) a year, one of the fastest spreading rates of any ridge. But the Pacific Ocean is actually getting smaller, not bigger. This is because crust is being subducted at an even faster rate along the edges of the ocean.

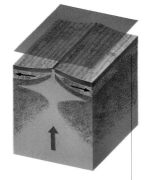

Fast-spreading ridges are usually quite low-lying. The runny lava builds a thinner crust than that found at slow-spreading ridges.

Profile of part of the Mid-Atlantic Ridge

Sea level
7,800 ft (2,400 m)
15,700 ft (4,800 m)

Slow-spreading ridges

The Carlsberg Ridge and the Mid-Atlantic Ridge spread at a much slower rate than the East Pacific Rise, at a speed of less than an inch (about 2 cm) a year. But over many years this makes quite a difference – when Christopher Columbus sailed across the Atlantic in 1492, the ocean was some 65 ft (20 m) narrower than it is today. The Mid-Atlantic Ridge is marked by a steep valley that runs down its center.

Slow-spreading ridges are much steeper and more jagged than those that spread quickly. The crust is also much thicker.

Transform fault
Fracture zone
PLATE A
PLATE B
Ocean ridge
PLATE A
Ocean ridge
PLATE B

Although there is little sediment on the ridge itself, a thick layer blankets the surrounding areas.

TRANSFORM FAULTS AND FRACTURE ZONES

As the mid-ocean ridges spread out, they cause collisions between the plates of the Earth's crust. Some collisions are head-on. Others occur at an angle, as the plates try to slide and scrape past rather than over each other. This slipping and sliding causes deep cracks, called transform faults and fracture zones, to appear in the ocean crust. Transform faults usually run at right angles to the center line (axis) of the ridge. Earthquakes are commonplace along them. Fracture zones are the remains of old, inactive transform faults.

Rift valley

THE SAN ANDREAS FAULT

The San Andreas Fault in California is a good example of a transform fault. It lies at an angle to an ocean ridge and forms the boundary where two plates are trying to slide past each other. In this case, the Pacific Plate is moving northwestward past the North American Plate. The movement of the plates triggers off frequent earthquakes. In 1906, the city of San Francisco was hit and largely destroyed by a particularly violent earthquake. In 1989, another terrible earthquake shook the city. No one knows when the next one will strike.

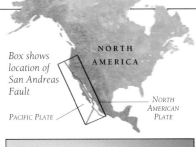

Box shows location of San Andreas Fault

NORTH AMERICA
PACIFIC PLATE
NORTH AMERICAN PLATE

Huge rock cracks mark the fault line, which is clearly visible from the air.

San Francisco
Los Angeles
NORTH AMERICAN PLATE
PACIFIC PLATE

Direction of plate movement

Ridges and rifts

The lava rising underneath a ridge is so hot that it melts some of the crust above it. This molten mass pushes upward, helping to open a deep crack called a rift along the middle of the ridge. Rifts run down the center of all mid-ocean ridges, marking the line of active seafloor spreading.

The Arctic Ocean

THE SMALLEST AND SHALLOWEST of the world's oceans is the Arctic Ocean. It covers an area of about 5,440,000 sq miles (14,089,600 sq km) and has an average depth of 4,265 ft (1,300 m), with a maximum depth of 17,880 ft (5,450 m) on the Pole Abyssal Plain. The Arctic Ocean is the only ocean to be almost entirely surrounded by land – Europe, Asia, Greenland, and North America. For most of the year, and particularly in the freezing winter months, its waters are covered by a thick sheet of ice. The North Pole, therefore, lies in the middle of a raft of ice, not on top of solid land. The ice cover has long been a challenge to ships. As a result, comparatively little is known about the area's oceanography. Despite its harsh conditions, people, such as the Inuit in Greenland, have lived around the edges of the Arctic Ocean for centuries.

The continental shelf
The Arctic Ocean has unusually wide areas of continental shelf. They lie under about a third of the whole ocean. Off the coasts of Greenland and North America the shelf is 50–124 miles (80–200 km) wide – about average. But to the north of Asia, where the shelf reaches its widest point, it is 994 miles (1,600 km) wide.

The Arctic Mid-Ocean Ridge
One of the major features of the Arctic seafloor is the Arctic Mid-Ocean Ridge. It is the northernmost extension of the Mid-Atlantic Ridge, located on the Asian side of the Pole Abyssal Plain, the deepest part of the ocean. It is one of three major ridges in the Arctic, and an active site of seafloor spreading.

The days are long in the Arctic summer.

In winter, the Sun barely rises.

Sun

The coldness of the Poles
At the Poles, the Sun's rays hit the Earth at a low angle. Their heat has to spread over a much larger area than it would at the Equator. Depending on the season, one or the other pole may be tilted away from the Sun, and can remain dark for months. Parts of the Arctic spend January and February in total darkness.

Arctic icebergs
The Arctic Ocean is littered with icebergs. About 90 percent of these have broken off the glaciers on the coasts of Greenland. Greenland itself lies under a huge ice cap, up to 1.8 miles (3 km) thick in some places.

ARCTIC CROSS-SECTION
The cross-section below shows the seafloor features found along the line A–B on the main map above.

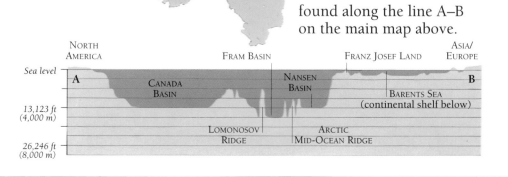

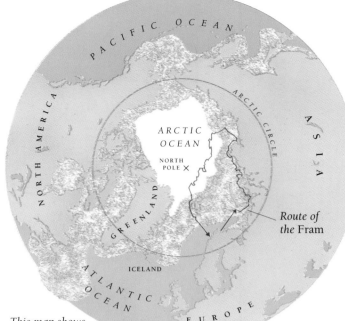

This map shows the farthest extent of pack ice. About half the ice melts in summer.

Polar ice (on the right) is usually flat, with raised edges. When the ice begins to thaw in summer, the water gnaws away at the underside of the edges. This creates the ragged shapes and deep cracks shown here.

THE FROZEN SEA

The ice covering the Arctic Ocean is called sea ice, because it forms from frozen seawater. There are three types of sea ice: polar ice, pack ice, and fast ice. Most of the ocean is covered in polar ice, which can be up to 164 ft (50 m) thick but melts to 6 ft 6 in (2 m) in summer. Pack ice forms around the edges of the ocean. Its maximum thickness is 6 ft 6 in (2 m). In winter, fast ice forms between the shore and the pack ice. It is called "fast" because it is attached firmly (or fast) to the shore. At its farthest extent, pack ice covers about 451,740 sq miles (11,700,000 sq km) of the ocean.

Arctic pack ice is broken and crushed together again by the endless movement of the water. This can result in fantastic ice formations such as those shown above.

Nansen designed the Fram (right) to drift with the ice without being crushed by it.

EXPLORING THE ARCTIC

In 1893, Norwegian scientist Fridtjof Nansen led an expedition to investigate claims that there was a solid continent of land at the Arctic. They took provisions to last five years. It was a wise precaution – their ship, the *Fram,* soon found itself frozen firmly into the ice near the New Siberian Islands. The ship drifted with the ice for three years, covering more than 994 miles (1,600 km) before breaking free. In 1958, a submarine, the USS *Nautilus,* traveled right under the ice cap, finally proving that there is no Arctic continent.

ARCTIC WILDLIFE

There is little wildlife in the middle of the Arctic Ocean, but around the edges it's a different story, especially in the summer when the ice melts. Then the algae that live in and under the sea ice bloom, providing food for fish such as the Arctic cod. The fish, in turn, are eaten by seabirds, seals, and some whales. Some animals, such as polar bears, are permanent residents. Others, such as blue whales, visit the Arctic in summer to feed and breed.

Map of migration route of Arctic tern

Arctic tern
This well-traveled bird makes the longest migration of any animal. It breeds in the Arctic during the brief summer. When winter comes, it flies to the opposite pole, to take advantage of summer in the Antarctic. Then during the Antarctic winter, it flies back to the Arctic – a round trip of more than 25,000 miles (40,000 km) each year.

Polar bear
Roaming across the ice and snow in search of its prey, the polar bear lives a nomadic life.

A fully grown male narwhal may be 20 ft (6 m) long, without the tusk.

Beluga whales can swim under the pack ice. If trapped, they sometimes break through by ramming their heads against the ice.

Walrus
Walruses gather in huge herds off the Arctic coast to breed. The males are enormous, with bristly whiskers and tusks up to 3 ft 3 in (1 m) long. They use these for self-defence, to root out shellfish, and to haul themselves out of the sea onto land. Walruses are insulated from the icy cold by a layer of blubber just beneath their tough skin.

Narwhal
This small whale lives in groups. A male narwhal (above) has a long, spiral tusk – actually a twisted, overgrown tooth – which may grow up to 8 ft 10 in (2.7 m) long. Although they catch their food underwater, narwhals, like all sea mammals, must surface for air. Once at the surface, the male can rest by laying his tusk on the edge of the ice.

Beluga whale
Adult beluga whales are pure white in color. They swim in small herds, hunting for fish. These beautiful creatures are nicknamed "sea parrots" because they make so many chirping, clicking, and whistling noises. Unlike other whales, they can turn their necks to look around them.

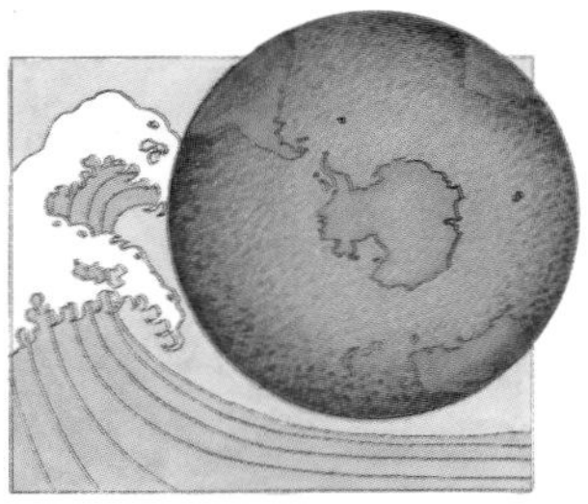

The Antarctic

AT THE OTHER END of the world from the Arctic lies the frozen continent of Antarctica, covered by a vast ice cap and surrounded by the freezing seas of the Antarctic Ocean. The Antarctic Ocean, which includes all the waters lying south of latitude 55°S, is the fourth largest of the world's oceans, covering an area of some 13,500,000 sq miles (35,000,000 sq km). In winter, more than half the Antarctic Ocean is covered with ice and littered with icebergs, which break off from the ice shelves at the edges of the continental ice cap. Even at the height of summer, Antarctica is fringed with sea ice. Unlike the Arctic, Antarctica is a continent of solid land. It has the coldest, windiest climate on Earth. Average winter temperatures along the coast are a bitter -22°F (-30°C); the temperature only rises above freezing in the brief southern summer, from December to March. Winds can reach more than 190 mph (300 km/h).

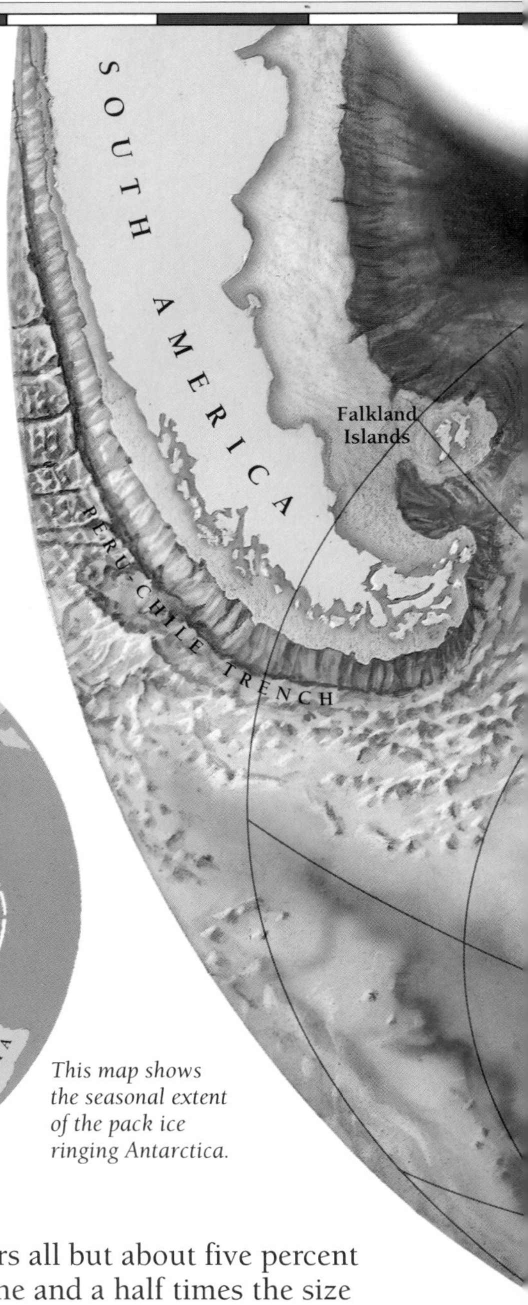

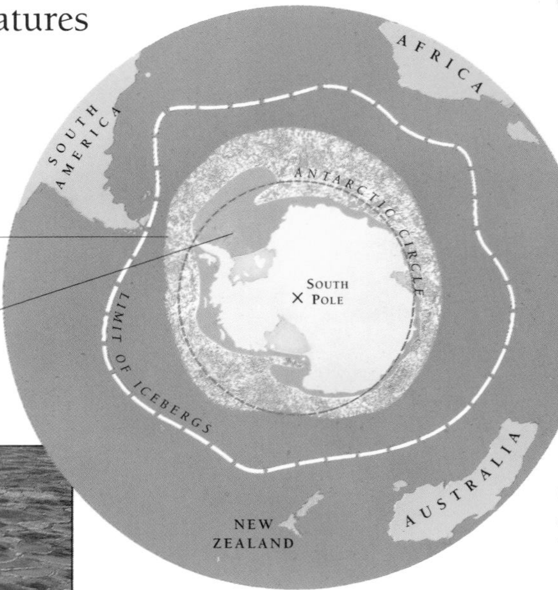

Pack ice in October

Pack ice in March

This map shows the seasonal extent of the pack ice ringing Antarctica.

LAND UNDER THE ICE

The outline on the map of Antarctica shows the edge of the ice cap that covers the land, not the land itself. The illustration below shows what the continent would look like if the ice cap were to be pulled away. The massive weight of the ice pushes much of the land below sea level, although the peaks of the Transantarctic Mountains break through the ice.

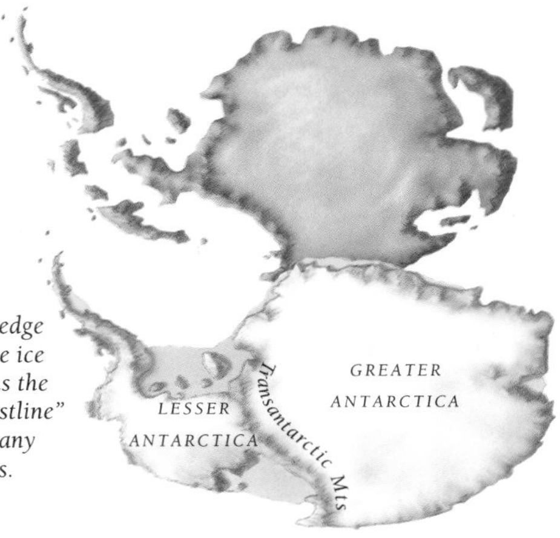

The edge of the ice forms the "coastline" in many areas.

GREATER ANTARCTICA

LESSER ANTARCTICA

Transantarctic Mts.

New sea ice forms in flat, round pieces called "pancake ice." A "pancake" may be up to 10 ft (3 m) in diameter.

THE DOME OF ICE

The vast sheet of ice that covers all but about five percent of the Antarctic continent is one and a half times the size of the US and up to 9,842 ft (3,000 m) thick. The ice cap, formed from frozen snow, has taken tens of thousands of years to accumulate, and contains an amazing 90 percent of all the ice on Earth. Without the weight of the ice, Antarctica would rise by 656-984 ft (200-300 m).

SOUTH GEORGIA

ICE SHELF

Sea level

6,561 ft (2,000 m)

SCOTIA SEA

WEDDELL ABYSSAL PLAIN

19,685 ft (6,000 m)

A

B

ANTARCTIC OCEAN CROSS-SECTION

The cross-section above shows a profile of some of the features on the Antarctic Ocean seafloor. It is taken along the line A–B on the main illustration.

ANTARCTIC WILDLIFE

The frozen wastes of Antarctica are largely deserted, but the Antarctic Ocean teems with life. This is made possible by the vast amount of plant plankton that grows in the icy sea in spring. It begins a food chain that links together krill, fish, seals, whales, and penguins. All of these have adapted to life in the world's freezer. Many Antarctic fish, such as plunderfish and other icefish, have a natural antifreeze in their blood.

Icefish

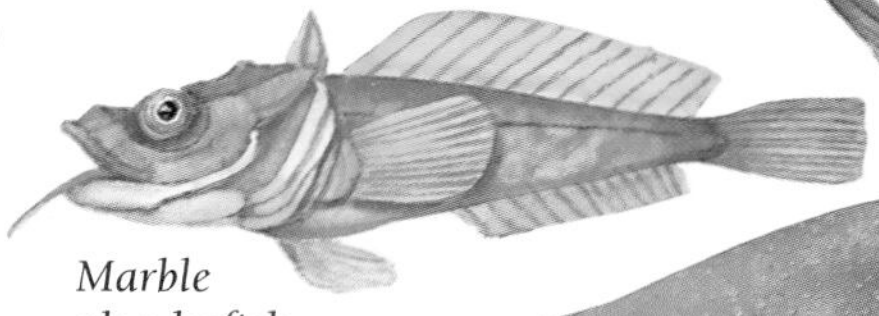

Marble plunderfish

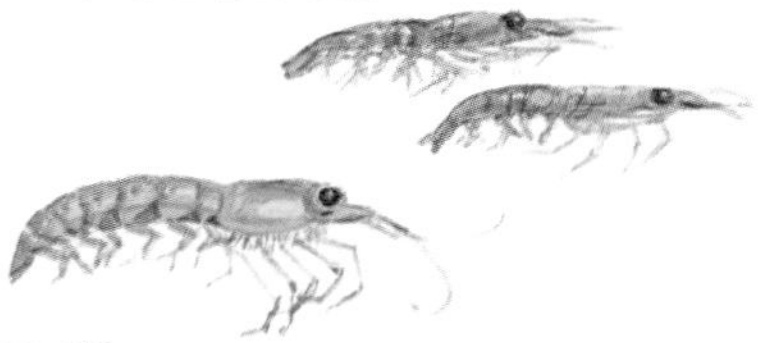

Krill

Krill are tiny shrimplike creatures, about 1½ in (4 cm) long. Despite their size, krill are the primary food source for a great number of species, including Antarctic whales, seals, squid, fish, and penguins. In summer, they form huge swarms, which appear as giant red patches on the ocean.

Each gulp of water is filtered for krill, then squeezed out.

Blue whale

In summer, a blue whale may eat up to 4.1 tons (4 tonnes) of krill a day. It filters seawater through baleen, the fringed plates hanging from the sides of its mouth. Blue whales are the largest animals alive today, weighing up to 132 tons (130 tonnes). Other Antarctic Ocean whales include humpback, sperm, and killer whales.

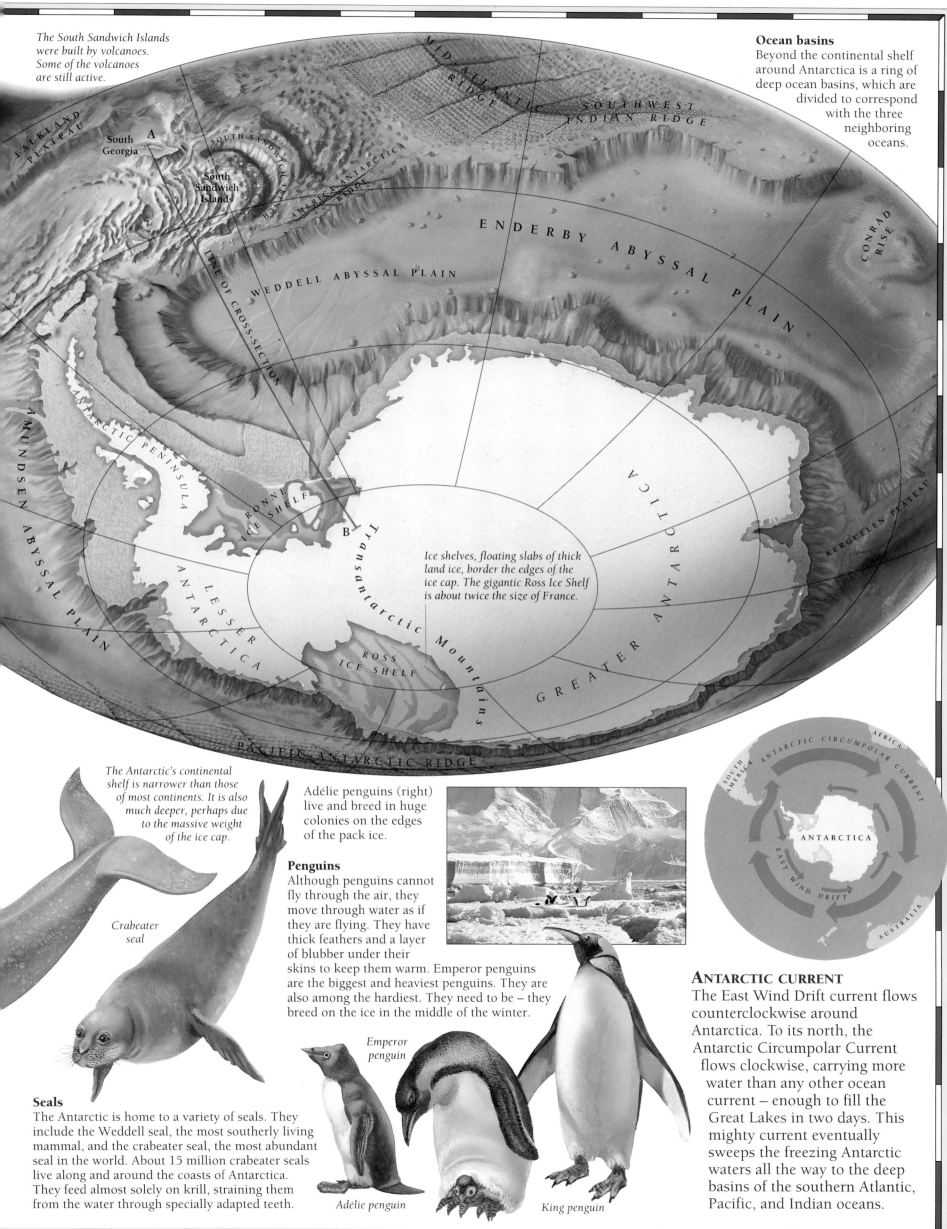

The South Sandwich Islands were built by volcanoes. Some of the volcanoes are still active.

Ocean basins
Beyond the continental shelf around Antarctica is a ring of deep ocean basins, which are divided to correspond with the three neighboring oceans.

Ice shelves, floating slabs of thick land ice, border the edges of the ice cap. The gigantic Ross Ice Shelf is about twice the size of France.

The Antarctic's continental shelf is narrower than those of most continents. It is also much deeper, perhaps due to the massive weight of the ice cap.

Adélie penguins (right) live and breed in huge colonies on the edges of the pack ice.

Crabeater seal

Penguins
Although penguins cannot fly through the air, they move through water as if they are flying. They have thick feathers and a layer of blubber under their skins to keep them warm. Emperor penguins are the biggest and heaviest penguins. They are also among the hardiest. They need to be – they breed on the ice in the middle of the winter.

Emperor penguin

Adélie penguin

King penguin

ANTARCTIC CURRENT
The East Wind Drift current flows counterclockwise around Antarctica. To its north, the Antarctic Circumpolar Current flows clockwise, carrying more water than any other ocean current – enough to fill the Great Lakes in two days. This mighty current eventually sweeps the freezing Antarctic waters all the way to the deep basins of the southern Atlantic, Pacific, and Indian oceans.

Seals
The Antarctic is home to a variety of seals. They include the Weddell seal, the most southerly living mammal, and the crabeater seal, the most abundant seal in the world. About 15 million crabeater seals live along and around the coasts of Antarctica. They feed almost solely on krill, straining them from the water through specially adapted teeth.

Winds and Waves

THE WATER IN THE OCEANS and the air in the atmosphere are closely linked. Wind is moving air, caused by differences in temperature and pressure around the Earth. The Sun's heat drives the winds, which, in turn, affect the surface of the sea. Surface currents (see page 46) are powered by the wind. It is the wind, too, that creates waves, the ripples of water that flow through the sea and break on the shore. The diagram on the right shows the general pattern of winds that blow over the Earth. Some winds were of special significance to sailors of the past. The doldrums, for example, are an area of very light winds near the Equator. Sailing ships could be stranded there for weeks on end. The trade winds, on either side of the Equator, were far more welcome. They blow strongly and constantly in the same direction.

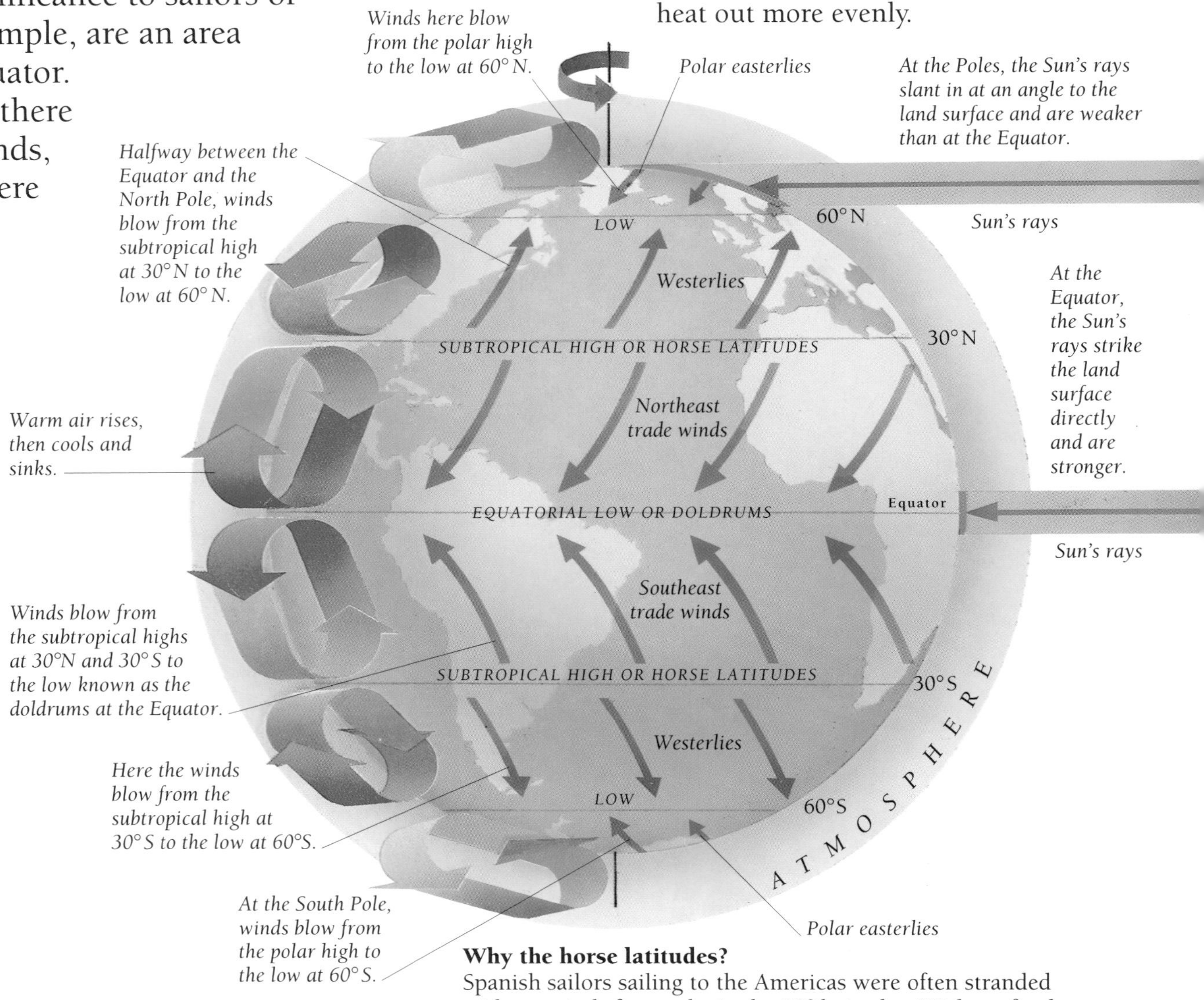

WORLD WINDS
At the Equator, the warm, light air rises, leaving an area of low pressure behind. Meanwhile at the Poles, cold, heavy air is sinking. It creates an area of high pressure. Air moves from high to low pressure, and this is what makes the wind blow. It does not blow in a straight line, however. It is swung to the side by the Coriolis Effect.

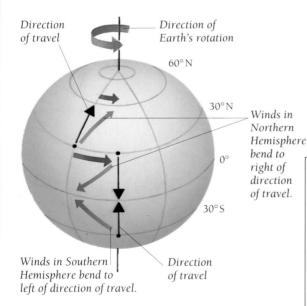

Direction of travel

Direction of Earth's rotation

60°N

30°N

0°

30°S

Winds in Northern Hemisphere bend to right of direction of travel.

Winds in Southern Hemisphere bend to left of direction of travel.

Direction of travel

THE CORIOLIS EFFECT
The direction that winds, currents, and weather systems travel is altered by the Earth spinning on its axis. This is called the Coriolis Effect. It causes winds, currents, and weather systems to swing to the right of the direction of travel in the Northern Hemisphere and to swing to the left of the direction of travel in the Southern Hemisphere.

HEAT BALANCE
The Sun heats some parts of the Earth's surface more than others. The Earth is hottest at the Equator where the Sun's rays strike directly and are concentrated in strength. The Poles are the coldest places on Earth because the Sun's rays strike at an angle and are, therefore, weaker. If nothing happened to correct the heat balance, the Equator would get hotter and hotter and the Poles colder and colder. Nothing would be able to survive in these regions. But the winds and ocean currents help to spread the heat out more evenly.

Winds here blow from the polar high to the low at 60° N.

Polar easterlies

At the Poles, the Sun's rays slant in at an angle to the land surface and are weaker than at the Equator.

Halfway between the Equator and the North Pole, winds blow from the subtropical high at 30° N to the low at 60° N.

LOW

60° N

Sun's rays

Westerlies

At the Equator, the Sun's rays strike the land surface directly and are stronger.

SUBTROPICAL HIGH OR HORSE LATITUDES

30° N

Warm air rises, then cools and sinks.

Northeast trade winds

EQUATORIAL LOW OR DOLDRUMS

Equator

Sun's rays

Winds blow from the subtropical highs at 30°N and 30°S to the low known as the doldrums at the Equator.

Southeast trade winds

SUBTROPICAL HIGH OR HORSE LATITUDES

30°S

Westerlies

Here the winds blow from the subtropical high at 30°S to the low at 60°S.

LOW

60°S

ATMOSPHERE

At the South Pole, winds blow from the polar high to the low at 60° S.

Polar easterlies

Why the horse latitudes?
Spanish sailors sailing to the Americas were often stranded without winds for weeks in the 30° latitudes. Without food, their horses starved, died, and were thrown overboard, giving the name "the horse latitudes" to this region.

LAND AND SEA BREEZES
Near the coast, the wind blows off the sea during the day and off the land at night. This is because during the day the land heats up more quickly than the water (top picture). Warm air rises and cooler air from out at sea blows in to take its place. At night, the pattern is completely reversed because the land cools down more quickly than the sea (bottom picture). Now the breeze blows off the land and out to sea. Land and sea breezes are the form of heating and cooling most easily experienced by anyone, as they occur on such a local scale.

Afternoon

Onshore breeze

Warm air rises off land

Night-time

Warm air rises off sea

Offshore breeze

WAVES

Waves are caused by the action of the wind blowing across the surface of the sea. Their steady progress across the open ocean is only broken when they reach the shore. The power of the waves lapping or pounding against the shore and the grinding action of any stones and pebbles they carry are constantly changing the shape of the world's coastlines. Wave height is measured from a wave's trough (lowest point) to its crest (highest point). Wave height is the vertical distance between the trough and the crest. Wavelength is the horizontal distance between two crests.

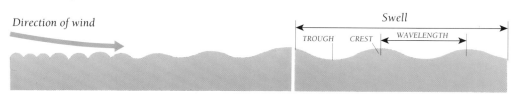

Direction of wind

Swell

TROUGH   CREST   WAVELENGTH

Open ocean The wind blowing across the open sea sets small, rounded waves in motion. If the wind continues to blow, these waves become longer and steeper. If the wind stops blowing, they form a steady swell.

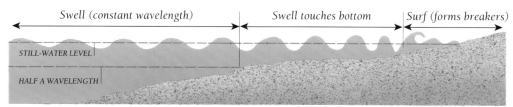

Swell (constant wavelength)   *Swell touches bottom*   *Surf (forms breakers)*

STILL-WATER LEVEL

HALF A WAVELENGTH

Surf zone As the waves near the shore, the water becomes shallower. When it is less than half a wavelength deep, the waves pile up. Then they topple over and "break" on the shore.

WAVE SIZES

The size of a wave depends on the wind speed, the length of time the wind blows (wind duration), and the distance over which the wind blows (the fetch). The stronger the wind and the longer it blows, the bigger the waves it creates. The highest recorded wave was 112 ft (34 m) high.

Fetch of wind (distance over which wind blows) affects size of waves

DIRECTION OF WIND

Refraction

If waves hit the shore at an angle, they may be bent so that they break almost parallel to the coast. This process is called refraction.

Wave refraction

WATER IN WAVES

The particles of water that make up a wave do not move forward with the wave. The wave moves through the water, like a ripple passing through a rope if you give it a shake. As a wave passes, each particle of surface water moves in a circle, then returns to its original position. An object such as a bottle will bob up and down, but only slowly move in any direction. Farther down in the water, particles move in smaller and smaller circles, stopping at a depth equal to half a wavelength.

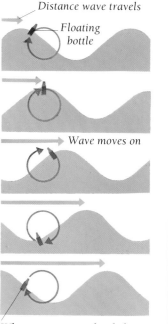

Distance wave travels

Floating bottle

Wave moves on

When wave passes, bottle has only moved a short distance.

Headlands

Wave action on rocky coasts can cause the erosion of headlands and produce caves and arches in the cliffs.

Surf

As waves near the shallow water of the coast, they slow down and bunch together. Wavelength gets shorter but wave height increases. When the waves are steep enough, they break on the shore in a rush of surf. Surf waves are called breakers, and come in three main types: spilling, plunging, and surging. Which type of breaker forms depends on the wind direction and kind of coastline.

Waves pile up, topple over, and break on beach.

Hawaii is famous for its spilling breakers, which attract surfers. Spilling waves are formed when incoming waves pile up over a gently sloping bottom, then break slowly on the beach over a wide area.

The Hazardous Sea

THE OCEANS PLAY A CRUCIAL PART in the world's weather and are the site of some of the most dramatic and destructive of all weather events. Immense, circular storms called hurricanes are born over warm, tropical seas. Huge waterspouts hang down from clouds, like small tornadoes. They were once mistaken for sea monsters by alarmed sailors. Other natural phenomena make the sea an even more hazardous place. Tsunamis race across the ocean faster than express trains, rearing up when they reach land to drown harbors and islands. Toward the North and South Poles, ice patrols keep a lookout for icebergs and disintegrating pack ice. Sea fog is another problem as it can reduce visibility and make navigation difficult.

HURRICANES

The name hurricane is taken from the Carib Indian word *hurrican*, which means evil spirit. Hurricanes are gigantic, spinning storms up to 298 miles (480 km) wide with winds blowing from 75 mph (120 km/h) to extremes of 145 mph (233 km/h). Hurricanes form over tropical seas. Warm, moist air is drawn upward and condenses to form rain. As it does so, it releases huge quantities of heat energy which fuel the hurricane. The warm air spins as it rises because of the Earth's twist. Cold air rushes in below to replace it. As the cold air is heated, it too rises and spins.

Rings of cumulonimbus clouds form around the center of a hurricane.

The eye of the hurricane is a calm area surrounded by a wall of clouds and whirling winds.

Eye of the hurricane

Winds rotate counterclockwise and spiral around the eye of the storm.

Direction of hurricane

BAHAMAS

FLORIDA

CUBA

JAMAICA

CARIBBEAN SEA

Direction of strong surface winds

Martinique

LESSER ANTILLES

THE BEAUFORT WIND SCALE

The Beaufort Scale was invented by Admiral Sir Francis Beaufort of the British Royal Navy in 1805. It was intended as a means of calculating wind speeds at sea. The scale was later modified for use on land.

Scale	Wind description	Conditions at sea
0	Calm	Smooth as a mirror
1	Light air	Ripples form
2	Light breeze	Small, short wavelets
3	Gentle breeze	Large wavelets; some foam
4	Moderate breeze	Small waves; white horses
5	Fresh breeze	Medium waves; some spray
6	Strong breeze	Larger waves; more foam crests can be seen
7	Strong wind	Sea heaps up; foam blown into streaks by wind
8	Fresh gale	Longer, higher waves; thick streaks of foam
9	Strong gale	High waves; crests of waves start to topple over; spray
10	Storm	Very high waves; sea looks white; poor visibility
11	Violent storm	Extremely high waves hide small ships from view; foam and froth cover sea surface
12	Hurricane	Air filled with driving spray and foam; violent waves

SOUTH AMERICA

ASIA

NORTH AMERICA

EUROPE

Tropic of Cancer

AFRICA

INDIAN OCEAN

PACIFIC OCEAN

CARIBBEAN SEA

Equator

SOUTH AMERICA

AUSTRALIA

Tropic of Capricorn

ATLANTIC OCEAN

Where hurricanes occur and why

Hurricanes are powered by heat, so they can only form over warm seas where the water temperature is at least 81°F (27°C) – roughly the area between the Tropics of Cancer and Capricorn. The storms run out of steam as they move over land or colder water. They are known by various names – hurricanes in the Caribbean, cyclones in the Indian Ocean, and typhoons in the northwest Pacific. The storms can cause great damage. Each year's storms are given individual names from an alphabetical list. The arrows on the map above show paths typically taken by hurricanes.

A hurricane strikes the island of Martinique.

Predicting hurricanes
In the countries worst hit by hurricanes, satellites are used to track the storms' paths. A storm warning can then be issued and people evacuated from the danger area. But it is difficult to track a hurricane exactly. So, aircraft are flown into the "eye" of the storm – the large, calm area in the center. They "seed" the clouds with silver iodine, salt, or silver crystals in an attempt to create another eye and divert the storm track. The picture above shows Hurricane Elena, photographed from the space shuttle *Discovery* in 1985.

Once a hurricane forms it generally moves westward, following the tropical trade winds.

Direction of hurricane

WATERSPOUTS
Waterspouts are whirling funnels of air which hang down from the base of cumulus or cumulonimbus clouds. When the twisting air touches the sea below, it sucks up a column of water and spray. Waterspouts are most common in warm, tropical seas. They can be 980 ft (300 m) wide and hundreds of feet (meters) high. A waterspout travels across the sea with its cloud. It rarely lasts for longer than 15 minutes. If the column of water is released suddenly, it can be devastating for ships and coastal areas.

Whirling air drops from cloud and touches down on sea surface.

Water sucked up by spinning column of air.

This waterspout formed off the coast of southern California in December 1969. It was 2,950 ft (900 m) high. When it collapsed, it killed three people and destroyed many buildings along the beach, including the pier, shown in the foreground.

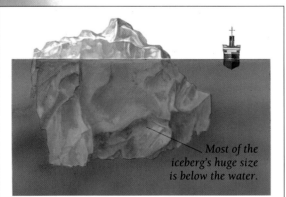

Most of the iceberg's huge size is below the water.

ICE AND FOG

Icebergs are found in the Arctic, North Atlantic, and Antarctic Oceans where they break, or "calve," off ice sheets and glaciers. Only a fraction of the berg shows above the water, as in the picture above, making it extremely hazardous to ships. Sea fog occurs when warm, moist air hits colder water. Fog reduces visibility and is doubly dangerous because it is so unpredictable. It can happen anytime, day or night, and lasts for a few hours or several days at a time.

TSUNAMIS
Tsunamis are triggered by underwater earthquakes or volcanoes. This causes the surrounding sea to bulge and then spread out in a series of ripplelike waves. As the waves travel through the open ocean, they can reach over 124 miles (200 km) in length, but are rarely more than 20 in (0.5 m) high. They move very fast though, at speeds over 435 mph (700 km/h). Tsunamis can pass by ships without being noticed. The real problem comes when they reach land. Then they slow down and rear up into huge waves, over 98 ft (30 m) high, which crash down, causing terrible destruction.

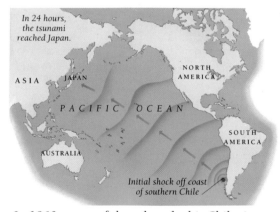

In 24 hours, the tsunami reached Japan.

ASIA JAPAN NORTH AMERICA PACIFIC OCEAN AUSTRALIA SOUTH AMERICA

Initial shock off coast of southern Chile

In 1960 a powerful earthquake hit Chile, in South America. The tsunami ripped across the Pacific, causing massive damage in Japan.

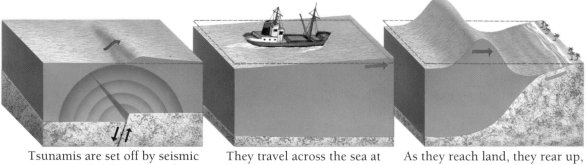

Tsunamis are set off by seismic activity under the water. They are not windblown waves.

They travel across the sea at high speed in a series of very long but very low ripples.

As they reach land, they rear up, sucking up water. Then they crash forward onto the shore.

Currents

THE WATER IN THE OCEANS is never still. It moves in waves and tides, and in enormous belts of water called currents. There are two main types of ocean currents – surface and deep water. Surface currents are swept along by the wind. These great "rivers in the sea" may be more than 50 miles (80 km) wide and flow at speeds of 136 miles (220 km) a day. Some of these currents are huge. The West Wind Drift, which flows around Antarctica, carries about 2,000 times as much water as the Amazon River.

Surface currents may be as warm as 86°F (30°C) or as cold as 30°F (-2°C). They have a profound effect on the world's weather, helping to spread the Sun's heat around the globe. The winds also help distribute the Sun's heat. Without winds and currents, the poles would get colder and colder and the tropics hotter and hotter. The second main type of current is deep-water flow. In this case, the water moves because of differences in density (see below).

SKIMMING THE SURFACE

In the open ocean, wind-driven surface currents move in large, roughly circular patterns. These are called gyres. They circulate in a clockwise direction in the Northern Hemisphere, and in a counterclockwise direction in the Southern Hemisphere. There are two large gyres in the Northern Hemisphere, and three in the Southern Hemisphere.

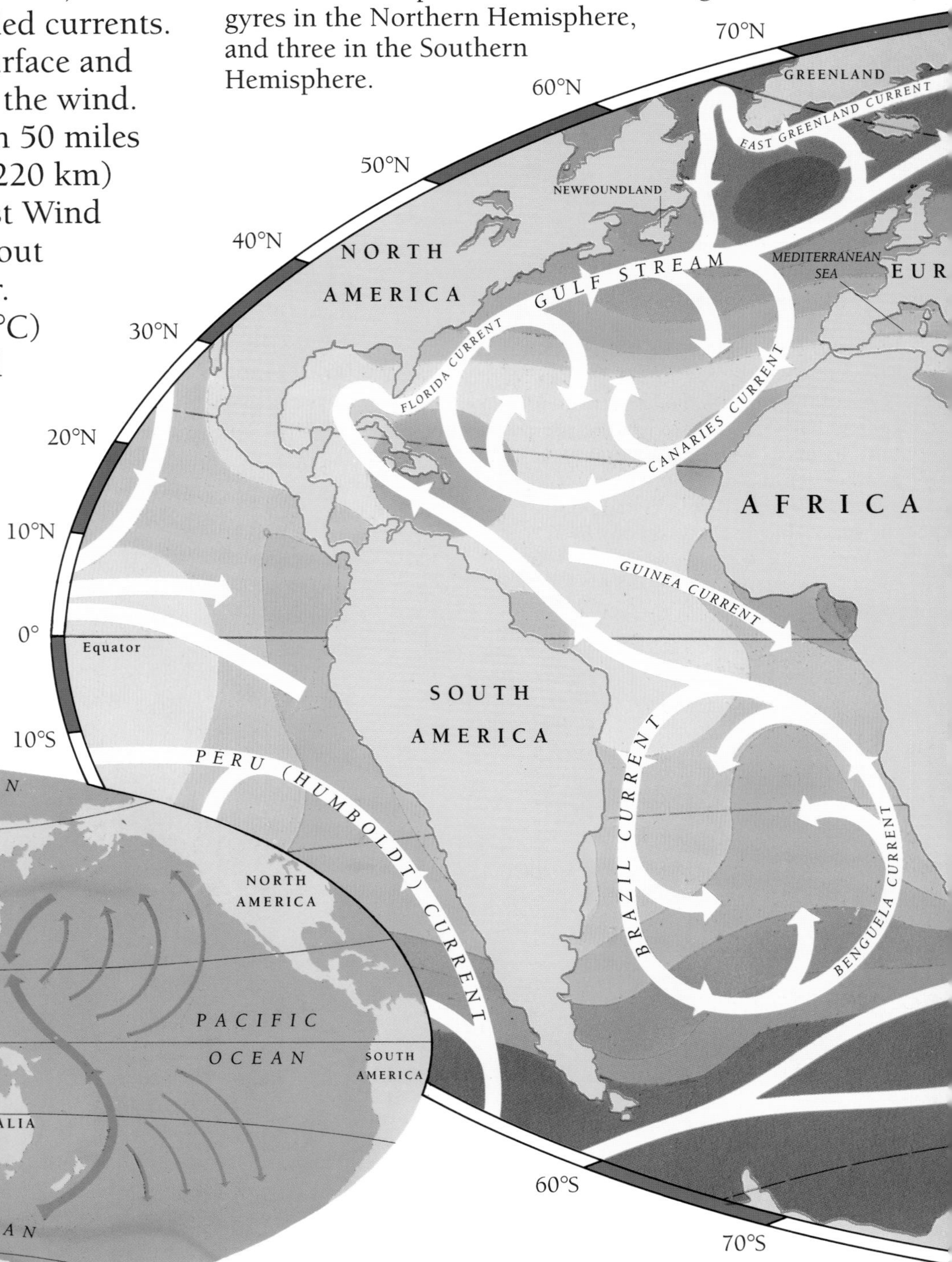

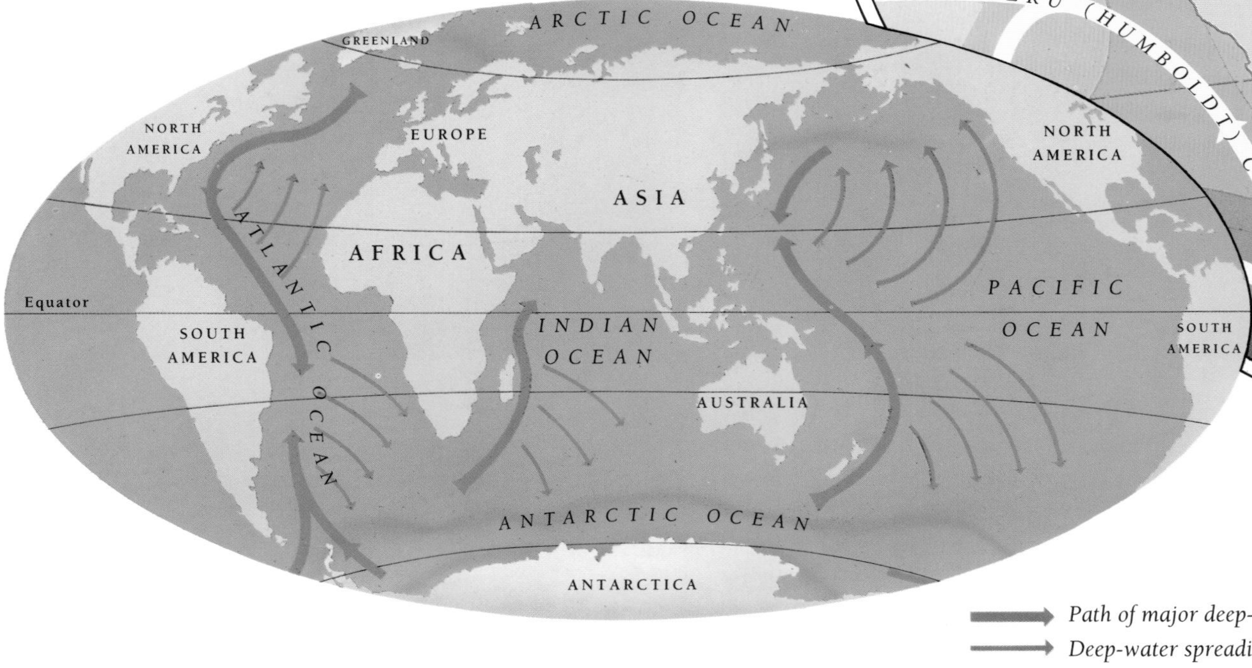

Path of major deep-water currents
Deep-water spreading

DEEP-WATER FLOW

Deep-water currents are set in motion by differences in the density of seawater. The colder and saltier water is, the greater its density. Under the ice shelves at the poles, the water is very cold and weighted down with salt, which has drained in from the ice. The dense water sinks into the deep sea, as shown in the diagram on the right. Warmer, less dense water flows in to replace it closer to the surface. This type of ocean circulation is called thermohaline. "Thermo" means temperature and "haline" means saltiness. Dense water forms mainly in Antarctica and in the north Atlantic Ocean near Greenland (shown on the map above). From there, the water sinks and spreads outward toward the Equator. The water moves very slowly – just a few feet (meters) a day.

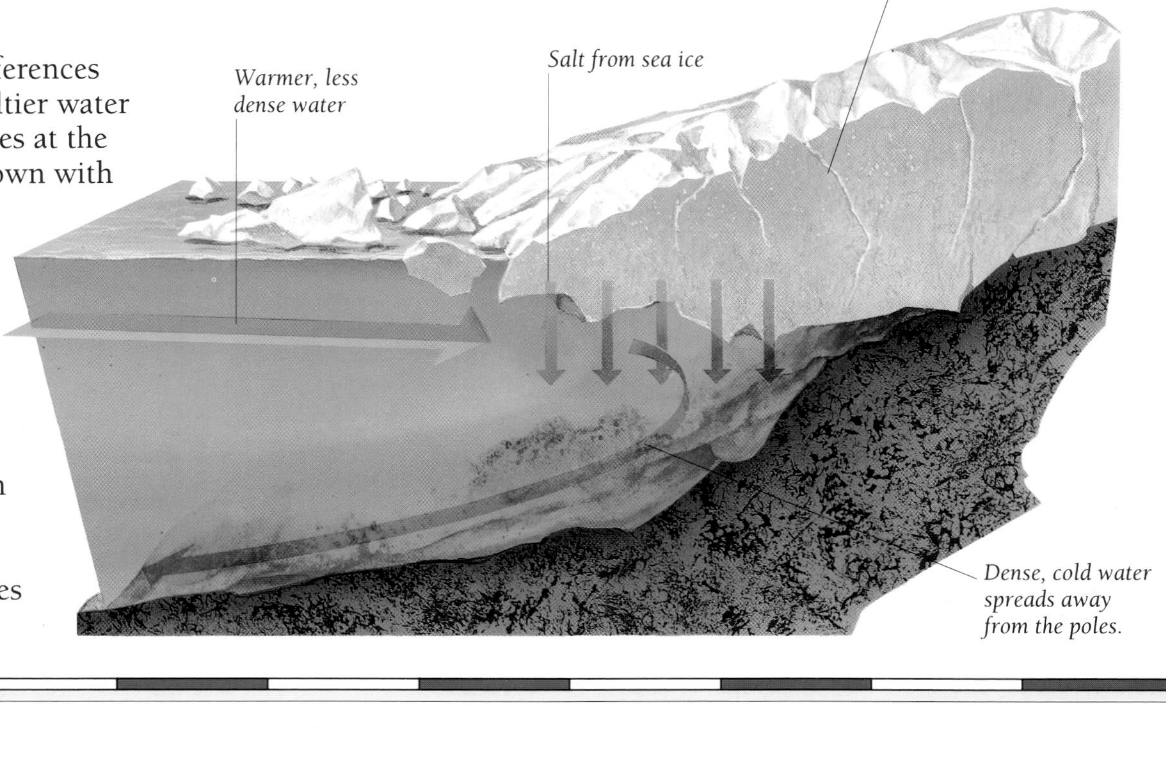

Warmer, less dense water

Salt from sea ice

Ice shelf

Dense, cold water spreads away from the poles.

The Gulf Stream
The Gulf Stream is one of the world's best-known warm currents. It was first noted in the 17th century, when shivering sailors off the coast of Newfoundland suddenly found their ships surrounded by warm water.

This photograph (right) shows a pattern of small circular currents, called eddies, in the Mediterranean Sea.

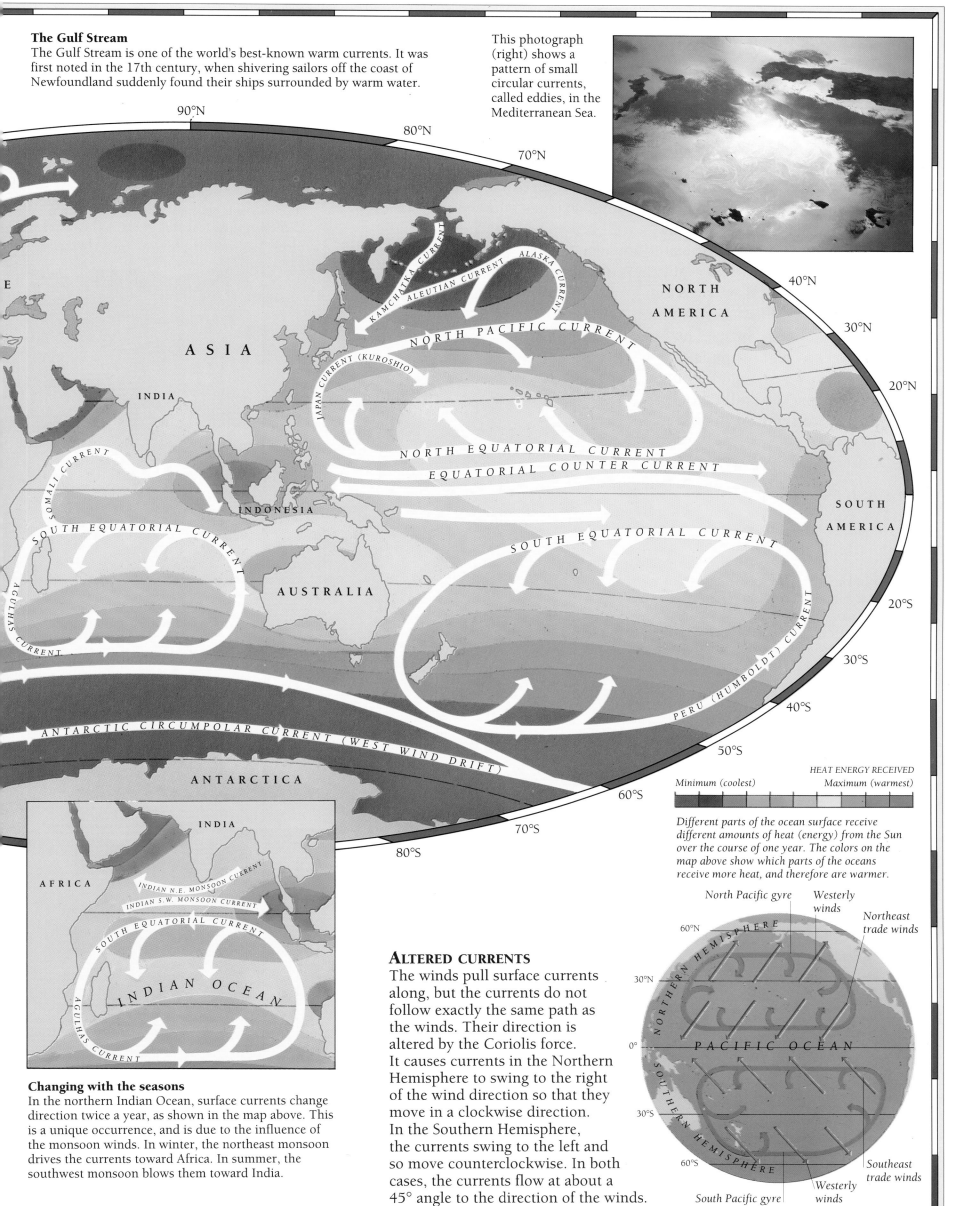

Different parts of the ocean surface receive different amounts of heat (energy) from the Sun over the course of one year. The colors on the map above show which parts of the oceans receive more heat, and therefore are warmer.

HEAT ENERGY RECEIVED
Minimum (coolest)   Maximum (warmest)

Changing with the seasons
In the northern Indian Ocean, surface currents change direction twice a year, as shown in the map above. This is a unique occurrence, and is due to the influence of the monsoon winds. In winter, the northeast monsoon drives the currents toward Africa. In summer, the southwest monsoon blows them toward India.

ALTERED CURRENTS
The winds pull surface currents along, but the currents do not follow exactly the same path as the winds. Their direction is altered by the Coriolis force. It causes currents in the Northern Hemisphere to swing to the right of the wind direction so that they move in a clockwise direction. In the Southern Hemisphere, the currents swing to the left and so move counterclockwise. In both cases, the currents flow at about a 45° angle to the direction of the winds.

Changing Sea Levels

THE LEVEL OF THE SEA CHANGES daily because of incoming and outgoing tides, waves, floods, and storm surges. But the changes are not very great, nor do they last very long. Over millions of years, the average level of the sea rises and falls much more, and for much longer. These long-term changes have been caused by the various ice ages and the periods of warmer weather between them. As ice sheets covered the Earth, they locked up huge amounts of water, lowering sea levels around the world by as much as 330 ft (100 m). When the ice melted, sea levels rose again. Sea level has risen by about 4½ in (12 cm) in the last 100 years. Of course, a change in sea level is relative to the level of the land. So, there are two ways sea level can change: the rise and fall of the land, and the rise and fall of the sea itself.

This raised beach is in Morro Bay on the Pacific Ocean coastline of California.

RISE AND FALL OF THE LAND

Sea level may seem to rise or fall because land levels change. The illustration below shows how this happens. The land level can change as a result of movements in the Earth's crust. For example, when an oceanic plate is subducted, the continental plate rises. The land can also be lifted when ice caps melt. During the ice ages, enormously heavy sheets of ice, some up to 9,842 ft (3,000 m) thick, covered the land, pressing it down. When the ice melted, the land began to rise. This is called isostatic change. It takes time for the land to return to its previous level. In Sweden, where the ice was once thick, the land is still rising at a rate of about ⅘ in (2 cm) a year.

PROOF OF SEA CHANGES

There is evidence that sea levels were once lower than today, but have risen. For example, freshwater sediment left by ponds and marshes has been found on continental shelves now covered by the sea. We can tell that sea levels have risen in the last 5,000 years, because the bones and teeth of land-living animals, such as mammoths and horses, have been found along coasts that are now under water. Geographical features such as those shown below also point to sea changes.

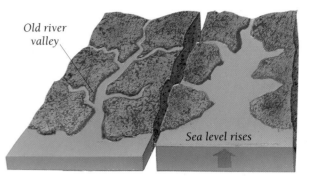

Old river valley

Sea level rises

Drowned valleys

If sea level rises, or the land sinks, the sea floods low-lying areas along the coast. Where the sea has flooded river valleys, it forms branching features called rias, or drowned valleys. The estuaries of southwest England are examples of these. They are evidence that sea levels were once lower than today.

Raised beaches

As sea level falls, or the land rises, old shorelines are sometimes left high and dry above sea level. These features are known as raised beaches. In some places, a staircase of raised beaches forms, one above the other. Raised beaches are found on several coastlines from the Arctic to the South Pacific.

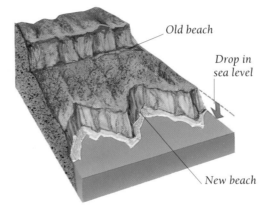

Old beach

Drop in sea level

New beach

Heavy ice presses on the Earth's surface, forcing it down.

When the ice melts, the water that is released causes the sea level to rise, but the land sometimes rises even faster.

The weight of the ice above pushes the crust downward and outward.

Melted blobs of oceanic crust rise up to join the continental crust, making the land higher.

At a subduction zone, the oceanic crust is driven down under the continental crust.

RISE AND FALL OF THE SEA

Sea level rises and falls when the volume of water in the oceans changes. These changes are called eustatic movements. They are often caused by seawater freezing or melting, in response to changes in the ocean temperature. A drop of 1½°F (1°C) in the temperature of the ocean can cause enough seawater to freeze to make the sea level drop by 6 ft 6 in (2 m). In the last 2,000 years, the Earth has been gradually growing warmer. Ice caps and glaciers have melted and the sea level has risen. The water in the oceans also expands as it gets warmer, and contracts when it gets colder.

THE WATER CYCLE

The Earth's water supply is constantly being recycled. The illustration on the right shows how the water cycle works. The Sun's heat evaporates millions of gallons (liters) of water from the Earth's surface – from the soil, green plants, oceans, lakes, and rivers. It rises into the air as water vapor, condenses to form clouds, and falls back to Earth as rain or snow. Some water falls directly into the oceans, rivers, and lakes; some soaks into the land and is taken up by plants or seeps into rivers. Then the whole water cycle begins again.

As air rises and cools, water vapor condenses into tiny droplets.

Water droplets join to form clouds, which release water as rain and snow.

Water evaporates from the surface of oceans, lakes, and rivers.

Water falling on the land returns to the seas and lakes in rivers, or seeps under the ground.

Carbon dioxide and other gases in the atmosphere keep the Earth warm by trapping some of the Sun's heat and preventing it from escaping back into space.

GLOBAL WARMING

For millions of years, carbon dioxide in the air has helped trap heat close to the Earth's surface, making it warm enough for life to survive. This is called the "greenhouse effect." When we burn fossil fuels (oil, coal, and gas), we add to the amount of carbon dioxide in the air. Other activities release different types of "greenhouse gases," which also increase this effect. Some scientists think that too much heat is being trapped and the Earth is getting too warm, too fast.

WORLDWIDE EFFECTS

If the Earth gets even a couple of degrees warmer, the effects could be devastating. Ice at the Poles could melt, raising sea level and flooding low-lying land along the coasts. Global warming could also disrupt weather patterns around the world, ruining harvests and increasing the risk and intensity of storms.

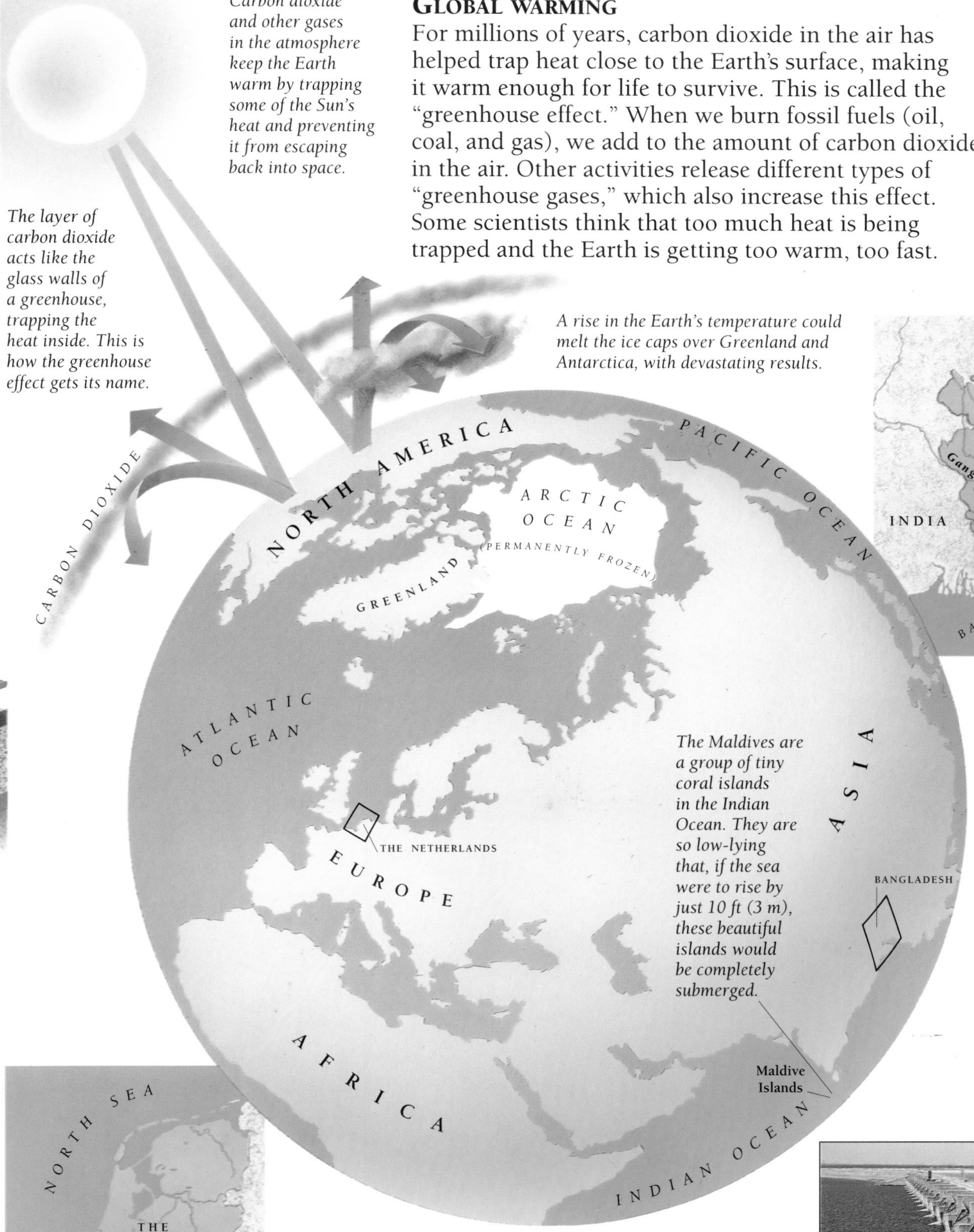

The layer of carbon dioxide acts like the glass walls of a greenhouse, trapping the heat inside. This is how the greenhouse effect gets its name.

A rise in the Earth's temperature could melt the ice caps over Greenland and Antarctica, with devastating results.

CARBON DIOXIDE

NORTH AMERICA

PACIFIC OCEAN

ARCTIC OCEAN (PERMANENTLY FROZEN)

GREENLAND

ATLANTIC OCEAN

A S I A

EUROPE

THE NETHERLANDS

BANGLADESH

AFRICA

The Maldives are a group of tiny coral islands in the Indian Ocean. They are so low-lying that, if the sea were to rise by just 10 ft (3 m), these beautiful islands would be completely submerged.

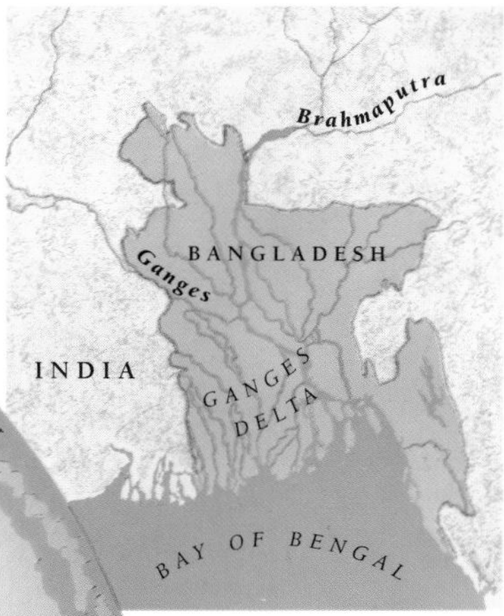

Maldive Islands

INDIAN OCEAN

Bangladesh

One of the areas most at risk from global warming is Bangladesh, in southern Asia. Most of Bangladesh is situated in the fertile but flood-prone Ganges Delta. A rise in sea level of just 3 ft 3 in (1 m) would destroy 14 percent of the country's crop-growing area.

Brahmaputra

BANGLADESH

Ganges

INDIA

GANGES DELTA

BAY OF BENGAL

This photograph shows the aftermath of a devastating flood that hit Bangladesh in 1991, killing many people and animals and ruining crops. About six percent of the country is permanently under water, and more than 60 percent of the total land area is flooded at some time of the year.

NORTH SEA

THE NETHERLANDS

The Eastern Scheldt Barrier

The Netherlands

The low-lying Netherlands has been at risk from flooding throughout its history. For many years, walls called dikes have been used to keep the sea at bay. But, as the Scandinavian landmass is rising, the Netherlands is sinking further. That, coupled with rising sea levels caused by global warming, could spell disaster.

The Eastern Scheldt Barrier is designed to keep the sea from flooding low-lying areas of the Netherlands. Without it, much land would be under water. But the barrier has had an effect on local marine life.

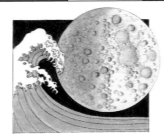

Tides

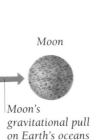

Earth's rotation

Moon

Earth

Moon's gravitational pull on Earth's oceans

TWICE A DAY, in most parts of the world, the sea rises and floods onto the shore. Twice a day it falls, or ebbs, away again. These daily changes in sea level are called the tides. They are caused mainly by the pull of the Moon and the Sun on the Earth. This pull makes the oceans wash back and forth across the Earth as though the water were in a giant bowl. Tides are also affected by the shape of the ocean basins, the shape of the nearby land, and by the Earth's rotation.

There are three types of tides. Which type occurs at a given location depends on many complex factors. Twice-daily, or semidiurnal, tides have two high and two low points each day. There is a six-hour interval. Daily, or diurnal, tides happen once a day, so there is only one high and one low tide each day. Mixed tides are a combination of the other two: there are two high and two low tides a day, but there can be a big difference in water height between the high tides in any one day.

TIDAL FORCE

The Moon's pull on the Earth's oceans is over twice that of the Sun. The diagram (left) shows how the Moon pulls the water into a bulge on the side of the Earth that faces it. To balance this, the Earth's rotation causes the water on the opposite side to pile up in a bulge, too.

SPRING AND NEAP TIDES

The tidal cycles take place over one lunar day, or 24 hours and 50 minutes. A second cycle, of spring and neap tides, happens over 28 days. Spring tides have the greatest range between high and low points. Neap tides have the smallest range. This is shown in the diagram below and on the right. This tidal cycle depends on the relative positions of the Moon, Sun, and Earth. There are two spring and two neap tides a month, about a week apart.

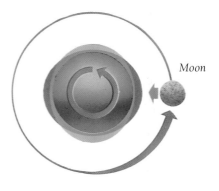

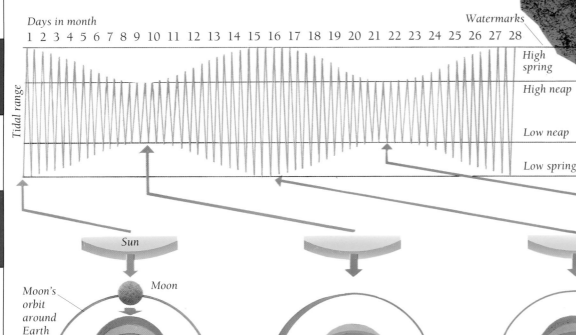

Days in month
1 2 3 4 5 6 7 8 9 10 11 12 13 14 15 16 17 18 19 20 21 22 23 24 25 26 27 28

Watermarks

High spring

High neap

Low neap

Low spring

Tidal range

Sun

Moon's orbit around Earth

Moon

Earth

Moon

Moon

Moon

New Moon
At the time of the new Moon, the Moon and Sun pull in a straight line. The tidal bulges combine to form a spring tide.

First quarter
In the first quarter, the Moon and Sun oppose each other. The two bulges nearly cancel each other, causing a neap tide.

Full Moon
The second spring tide in the month happens at the time of the full Moon. The Moon, Sun, and Earth are in a line again.

Third quarter
The second neap tide happens in the Moon's third quarter. The Moon, Earth, and Sun once again form a right angle.

TIDAL RANGES

The tidal range is the difference between the water height at high tide and low tide. On the open ocean coasts, the tidal range is usually between 6–10 ft (2–3 m). Seas that are almost surrounded by land, such as the Mediterranean, have hardly any tidal range at all. In some bays and river mouths, the tidal range can be as great as 56 ft (17 m). Strong winds can make tides higher or lower than normal. These surges can cause floods when high or increase the risk of ships grounding when very low.

The two pictures above show the difference in an estuary (a river mouth into which the sea flows) scene at low and high tide. At low tide (left), the sea has receded and the mud flats and the creatures that live on them are exposed. At high tide (right), the sea has rushed in and covered the mud flats to a considerable depth. The creatures that live at or below the tide line are covered by water.

Going up?
Ships in tidal harbors rise and fall with the tide. At low tide, they can be left high and dry as the water recedes.

Exposed zone
The high-tide zone is the highest and most exposed. Wildlife here may only be splashed, not fully covered, by the water.

Wet and dry
The mid-tide zone is the largest on the shore. It is submerged when the tide is in and exposed to the air when the tide goes out.

Under water
Plants and animals at the low-tide mark are usually covered by water even when the tide is out. But the water's temperature and salinity may vary when the tide is in.

HIGH-TIDE ZONE

MID-TIDE ZONE

LOW-TIDE ZONE

LIFE ALONG THE SHORE

Shoreline creatures have to survive being alternately submerged and exposed. They live in distinct zones, depending on how good they are at coping with drying out. Some animals hide in their shells or burrow in the wet sand to avoid drying up when the tide is out. Seaweeds are covered with a mucuslike protective coating, which keeps them moist. They are anchored to the rocks by their rootlike holdfasts, to prevent them from being swept out to sea.

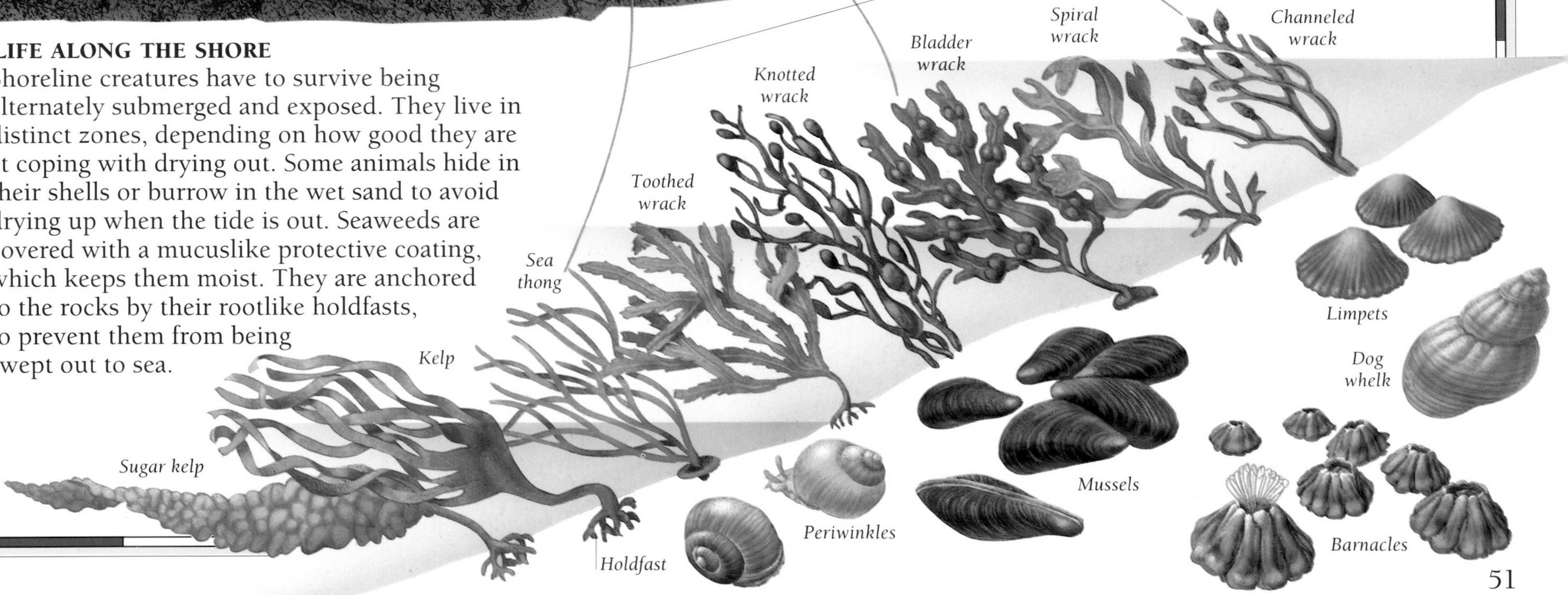

Spiral wrack

Channeled wrack

Bladder wrack

Knotted wrack

Toothed wrack

Sea thong

Kelp

Sugar kelp

Holdfast

Periwinkles

Mussels

Limpets

Dog whelk

Barnacles

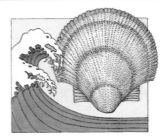

Fishing

FOR CENTURIES PEOPLE have caught fish from the sea for food. The first fishermen used spears, simple nets, and hooks – methods still used today. But fishing is also big business. About 74 million tons (75 million tonnes) of fish are caught each year, much of it by modern fleets using the latest equipment.

Only about 300 of the world's 20,000 species of fish are caught commercially. Two main kinds of fish are caught for food. These are called pelagic and demersal fish. Pelagic fish live near the surface of the sea, and demersal fish live on or near the seabed. Overfishing of some species is a serious problem. They are being taken from the sea too quickly for them to reproduce and keep their numbers up. Countries now set limits on the amount of fish caught. Apart from fish, the oceans' other food resources include shellfish, seaweed, sea cucumbers, and sea urchins.

COMMERCIAL FISHING

Commercial fishing fleets use the latest technology to locate fish and huge nets to catch them. Sonar is used to locate large schools. Pulses of sound are sent out from the boat and bounce back from the seabed below. If there is a school of fish nearby, the pulses take less time to return. The main types of nets used in commercial fishing are gill, or drift, nets, trawl nets, and purse seines. Apart from food fish, commercial fleets also catch other fish such as sand eels. This type is made into fish oil, and fish meal, which is used in animal foods.

These traditional fishermen from Kenya use net traps to catch fish.

ARTISANAL FISHING

Artisanal, or traditional, fishermen use a variety of equipment for catching fish and shellfish, including spears, handheld nets, rods and lines, fish traps, and pots. Traditional fishing boats range from dugout canoes to small motorized boats. Traditional methods require skill, and knowledge of the local tides and fish species. In many places, these skills are being lost as modern ships and technology replace them.

Up a pole
In Sri Lanka, fishermen sit on wooden stilts in the sea, fishing for sea bass and mullet with rods and lines.

Rock-wall traps
Traps made out of wood or stone strand schools of small fish as the tide goes out.

Pole fishing

Net skimming

Local fishing boat

Rock-wall trap

Cockle raking

Cockle raking
At low tide, cockles and other shellfish can be collected by hand or by raking the sand.

Net trap

Local craft
Small, local fishing boats can fish in waters that are too shallow for the larger fleets. They have small crews and their catches are usually sold close to where they are docked.

Net skimming
One type of net is skimmed over the shallow seabed to catch small fish and shrimps. The fisherman pushes the net in front of him, using two long poles.

Lobster pots
Wicker lobster pots are sunk to the seabed to catch bottom-dwelling lobsters, prawns, and crabs. Their positions are shown by floats on the surface of the sea.

Brown seaweed

Seaweed supply
Seaweed is harvested for food or fertilizer. It is also used as a source of vegetable gums, which are used to make ice cream and toothpaste.

Net traps
Some traps consist of a series of conical nets, with a cylinder at the end. They catch fish swimming with the current. They have large, net "wings" to guide the fish into the trap.

Lobster pot

Lobster (D)
20 in (50 cm)

Cockle (D)
Up to 2 in (5 cm)

At the end of a day's fishing, this boat's catch is transferred to shore for processing. Some larger trawlers process fish on board, cleaning and freezing their catch.

Purse seining

Purse-seine nets are used to catch whole schools of surface-living fish, such as tuna and sardines. The nets are so called because the ends are drawn together, as in a purse closing.

First the net is spread around the school of fish.

Then the two ends are pulled together, forming a large circle and the bottom of the net is closed, trapping the fish.

The net is drawn toward the boat and the fish are hauled out of it.

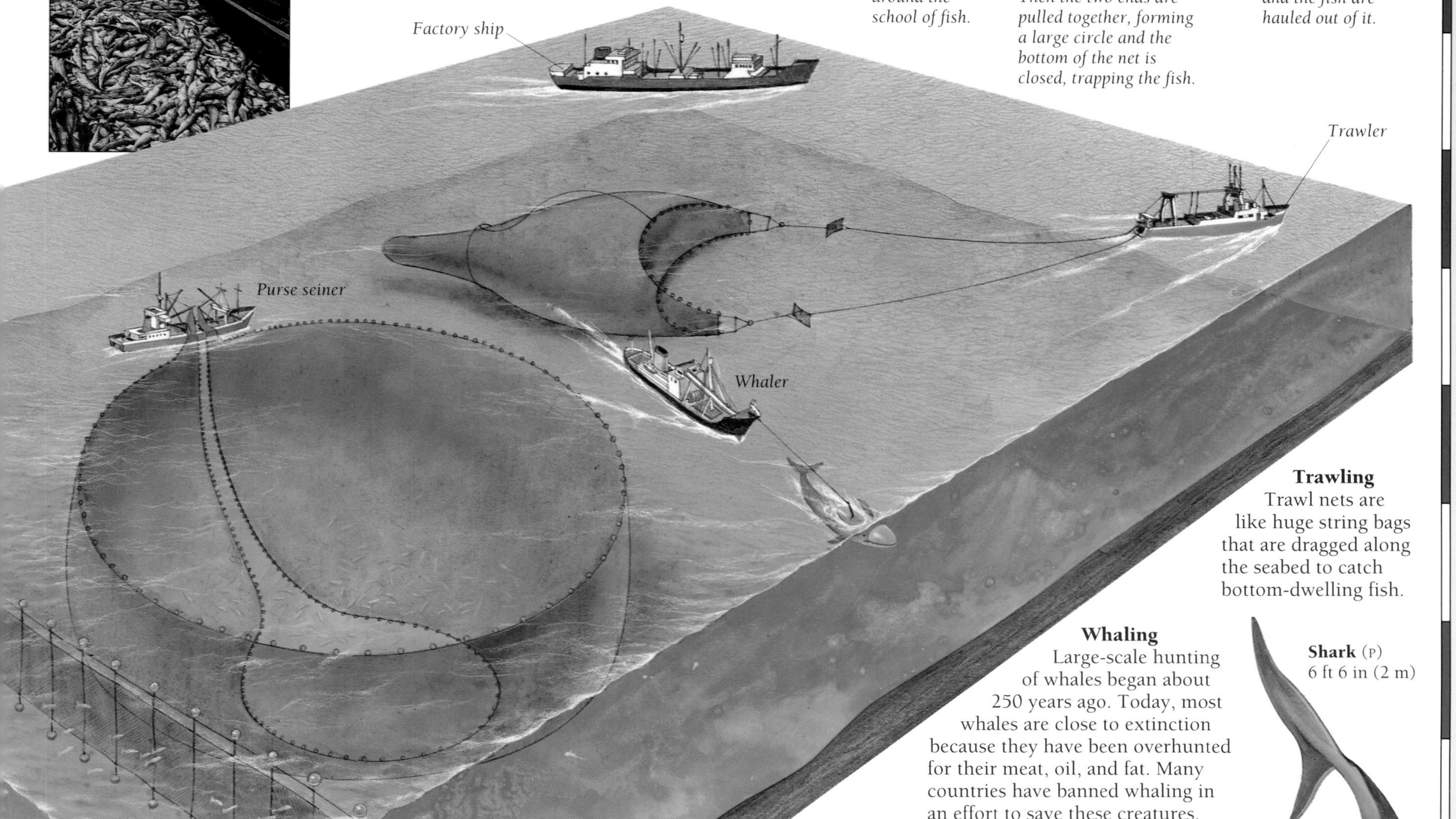

Factory ship

Trawler

Purse seiner

Whaler

Gill net

Trawling

Trawl nets are like huge string bags that are dragged along the seabed to catch bottom-dwelling fish.

Whaling

Large-scale hunting of whales began about 250 years ago. Today, most whales are close to extinction because they have been overhunted for their meat, oil, and fat. Many countries have banned whaling in an effort to save these creatures.

Shark (P)
6 ft 6 in (2 m)

Sardine (P)
8 in (20 cm)

Herring (P)
16 in (40 cm)

Pollack (P)
20 in (50 cm)

Sprat (P)
4 in (10 cm)

Mackerel (P)
16 in (40 cm)

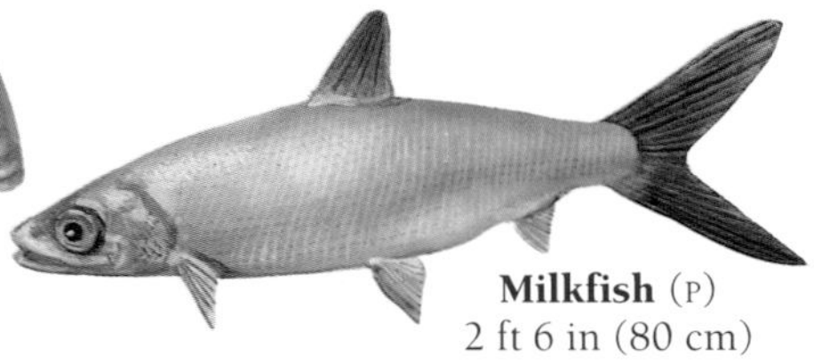

Milkfish (P)
2 ft 6 in (80 cm)

Cod (D)
3 ft 3 in (1 m)

Gill nets

Gill nets hang vertically under the sea, like huge curtains. They can be 12 miles (20 km) long. These nets drift with the tide. Apart from the fish they are designed to catch, they also snare and kill thousands of dolphins and seabirds each year.

Fish swim into the net, which is invisible underwater, and are trapped by their gills.

PELAGIC FISH

Pelagic fish (marked with P) live and feed near the surface of the sea. They include herring, mackerel, tuna, and sharks. Some important pelagic fish are shown here, along with their average sizes.

DEMERSAL FISH

Demersal fish (marked with D) live on or near the bottom of the sea. They include cod, haddock, plaice, flounder, prawns, and lobsters. Some important demersal fish are shown, along with their average sizes.

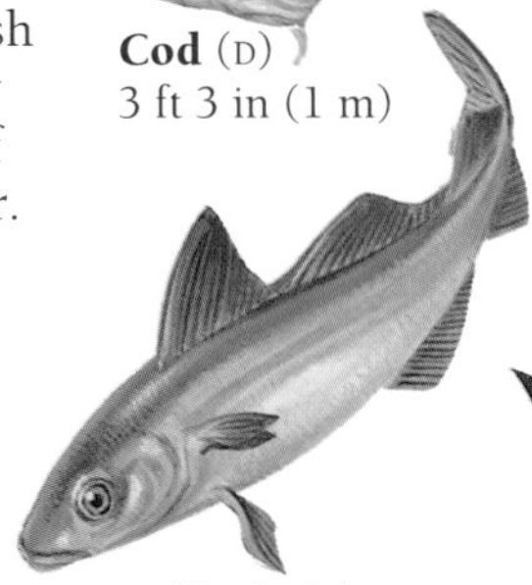

Haddock (D)
20 in (50 cm)

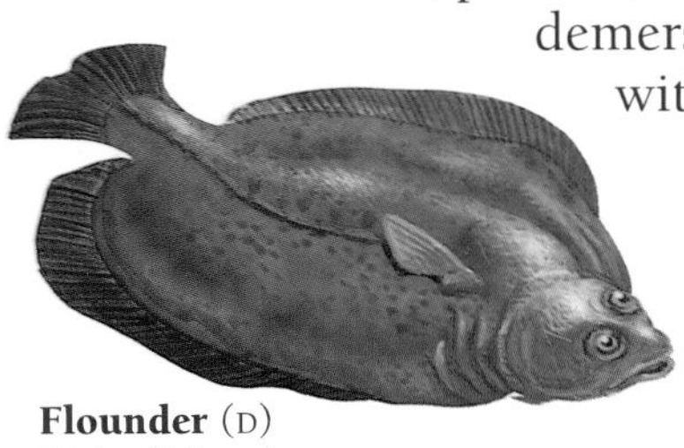

Plaice (D)
16 in (40 cm)

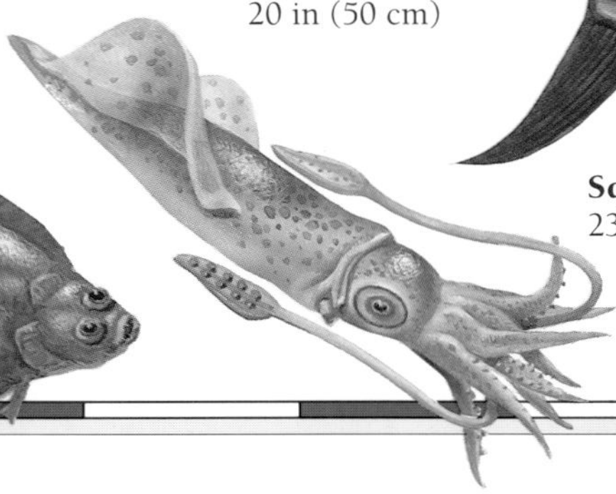

Squid (P)
23 in (60 cm)

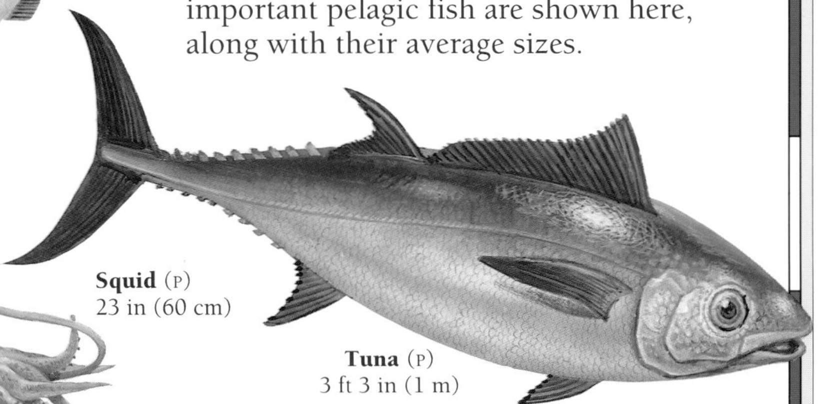

Tuna (P)
3 ft 3 in (1 m)

Flounder (D)
20 in (50 cm)

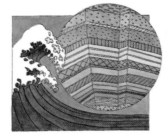

Oil and Gas

ABOUT ONE-FIFTH of the world's total supply of oil and natural gas comes from under the sea. The first offshore oil well was sunk in 1896 off the coast of California. Today, exploring and drilling for oil and gas at sea is a huge industry, employing millions of people and using the very latest technology.

Geologists first have to study the structure of seabed rocks to see if they contain oil or gas. But the only way to make sure is to drill a test hole. If oil is struck, production can begin and a more permanent platform is built, like the one shown in the large illustration. People and supplies are brought on board. As the oil or gas is extracted, pipelines carry it to the refinery. When as much oil as possible has been extracted, the well is sealed up. This is known as well "capping."

HOW OIL FORMS

Oil formed millions of years ago from the remains of prehistoric sea creatures. When they died, their bodies sank and were covered in layers of mud and sand, which slowly turned into layers of rock. The pressure of these layers and the action of bacteria turned the creatures' remains into thick oil. Natural gas formed in a similar way. Oil tends to move upward through soft rocks until it reaches a layer of harder rock and is trapped.

Derrick
The derrick is a steel tower that contains the drilling equipment.

Cranes
Cranes hoist supplies up to the platform.

Drill string
The drill string is made from lengths of steel pipe 33 ft (10 m) long. The drill bit is attached to the end.

Workers called "roughnecks" add sections to the drill string.

Fireboat
In the case of fire, fireboats can pump out thousands of gallons (liters) of water a minute at the fire.

1. The dead bodies of countless prehistoric sea plants and animals sank down to the seabed (arrows).

2. They were covered by mud and sand and turned to oil over millions of years. The oil moved up through soft layers of rock.

3. Oil gets trapped by hard layers of rock called "caprock," or by movements of the Earth's crust.

Steel jacket to support rig

Production wells

Production platform

Seabed

Oil-bearing rock squeezed by weight of rock above.

Oil tapped by production wells

Sharp teeth

"Drilling mud"

Drill bit
The drill bit rotates as it bites into rock. Its cutting teeth are made of steel or diamond. Drilling friction creates a lot of heat. Drilling fluid called "mud" is pumped down the drill string to cool the bit and to wash up the fragments of rock.

Production wells

To reach as much oil as possible, wells are drilled at different angles from one platform. Each wellhead is topped with a structure called a "Christmas tree" which is made up of valves and gauges.

LIFE ON A RIG

More than 100 people live and work on an oil rig. Food and other supplies are brought by boat from the shore, and rubbish is taken back to land for disposal. The rigs are often a long way from land. Workers may spend up to four weeks at a time on the rig.

Helicopters
Helicopters carry workers to and from the rig.

Landing pad

Flare stack
Any gas that rises with the oil and cannot be used is burned off. This is known as "flaring."

Lifeboats
Oil and gas are highly flammable. In a rig disaster, fireproof lifeboats give workers a chance of survival.

Fireproof lifeboat

Flare stack

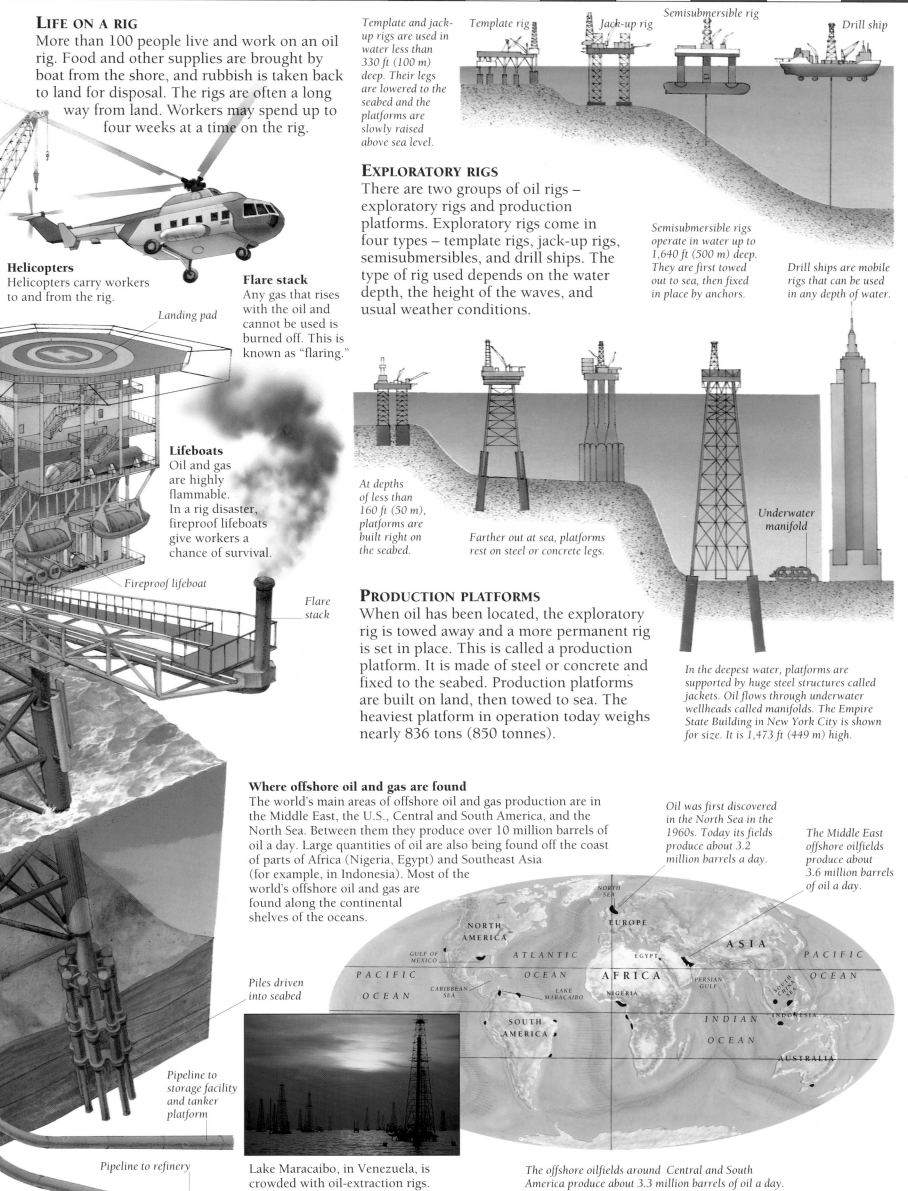

Template and jack-up rigs are used in water less than 330 ft (100 m) deep. Their legs are lowered to the seabed and the platforms are slowly raised above sea level.

Template rig   *Jack-up rig*   *Semisubmersible rig*   *Drill ship*

EXPLORATORY RIGS

There are two groups of oil rigs – exploratory rigs and production platforms. Exploratory rigs come in four types – template rigs, jack-up rigs, semisubmersibles, and drill ships. The type of rig used depends on the water depth, the height of the waves, and usual weather conditions.

Semisubmersible rigs operate in water up to 1,640 ft (500 m) deep. They are first towed out to sea, then fixed in place by anchors.

Drill ships are mobile rigs that can be used in any depth of water.

At depths of less than 160 ft (50 m), platforms are built right on the seabed.

Farther out at sea, platforms rest on steel or concrete legs.

Underwater manifold

PRODUCTION PLATFORMS

When oil has been located, the exploratory rig is towed away and a more permanent rig is set in place. This is called a production platform. It is made of steel or concrete and fixed to the seabed. Production platforms are built on land, then towed to sea. The heaviest platform in operation today weighs nearly 836 tons (850 tonnes).

In the deepest water, platforms are supported by huge steel structures called jackets. Oil flows through underwater wellheads called manifolds. The Empire State Building in New York City is shown for size. It is 1,473 ft (449 m) high.

Where offshore oil and gas are found

The world's main areas of offshore oil and gas production are in the Middle East, the U.S., Central and South America, and the North Sea. Between them they produce over 10 million barrels of oil a day. Large quantities of oil are also being found off the coast of parts of Africa (Nigeria, Egypt) and Southeast Asia (for example, in Indonesia). Most of the world's offshore oil and gas are found along the continental shelves of the oceans.

Oil was first discovered in the North Sea in the 1960s. Today its fields produce about 3.2 million barrels a day.

The Middle East offshore oilfields produce about 3.6 million barrels of oil a day.

Piles driven into seabed

Pipeline to storage facility and tanker platform

Pipeline to refinery

Lake Maracaibo, in Venezuela, is crowded with oil-extraction rigs.

The offshore oilfields around Central and South America produce about 3.3 million barrels of oil a day.

55

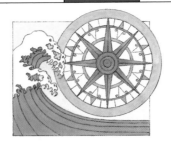

Shipping

FOR THOUSANDS OF YEARS, people have relied on ships for transport and trade. The first ocean explorers traveled in simple dugout canoes. Today's passenger-carrying ships include luxurious cruise liners, short-haul ferries, and speedy catamarans. As ships investigated and opened up the world, they also allowed distant countries to trade with each other. Most of the world's imports and exports are now carried by sea. Ships that carry goods and cargo are called merchant ships. They include container ships, bulk carriers, and the gigantic supertankers that transport oil (see below). Hundreds of kinds of ship are also involved in military duties and in the fishing industry.

The first ships and boats were rowed or paddled along. Sails were invented by the ancient Egyptians about 5,000 years ago. They remained the main driving force of ships until the mid-nineteenth century, when steam engines and propellers were developed. Most large ships today are powered by diesel engines.

SHIPPING ROUTES AND PORTS

The map below shows some of the world's main ports and shipping routes. Many of the ports grew up around the mouths of rivers. The world's busiest port is Rotterdam in the Netherlands. It is situated on the delta of the Rhine River. The set routes linking the major ports act like highways on land, and some parts are monitored to try to prevent collisions. The Suez and Panama canals are the most important shortcuts for ships.

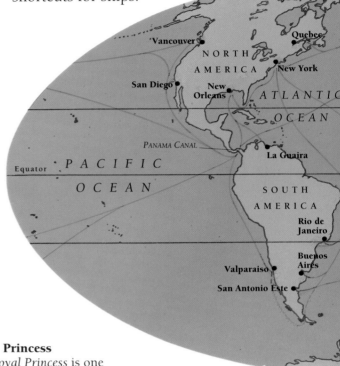

MODERN SHIPS

The ships shown below represent just a few of the many types of vessels using the sea today. Many are specially designed to carry cargo or passengers. Both can be carried long distances more cheaply by sea than by air. Some ships carry one type of cargo only; others carry a mixture. The world's fleet of merchant ships numbers more than 40,000 vessels. Other ships have specific functions, such as lifting extra-heavy objects, firefighting, or salvage work.

Passenger ferry
Nowadays most people prefer to go by airplane if they are traveling long distances. But passenger ferries are still in regular use on shorter trips. The largest ferry, in use in the Baltic Sea, can carry 2,500 passengers and 450 cars.

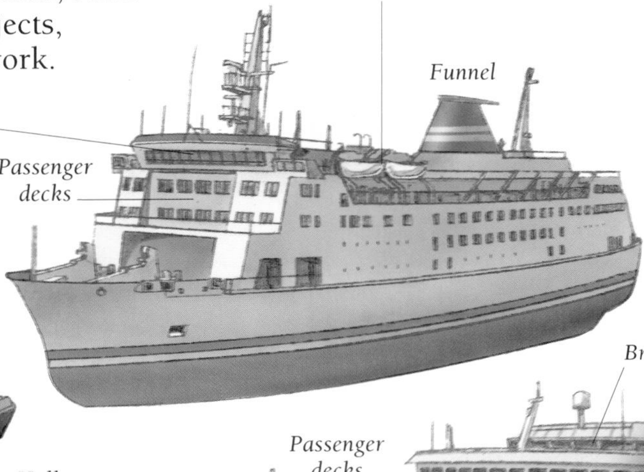

Royal Princess
The *Royal Princess* is one of the biggest cruise ships ever built. She sailed for the first time in 1984 from Southampton, U.K. to Los Angeles, U.S. The ship is like a floating hotel, with cabins for 1,200 passengers, a library, cinema, gymnasium, and four swimming pools.

Container ship
Container ships carry cargo in large metal boxes, or containers. The containers come in a range of standard sizes. They are designed to fit in the ship's hold or on deck and are loaded on by crane. The biggest container ships have room for 4,000 containers.

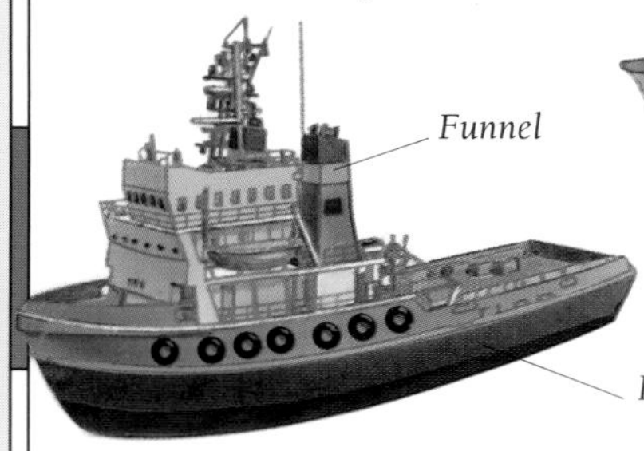

Bridge
The ship is navigated (steered) from here.

Passenger decks

Funnel

Funnel

Hull

Seagoing tug
Tugs are powerful boats, used for a variety of purposes. Some tow larger ships and guide them through difficult or dangerous waters. Others are used for repairing and servicing oil rigs.

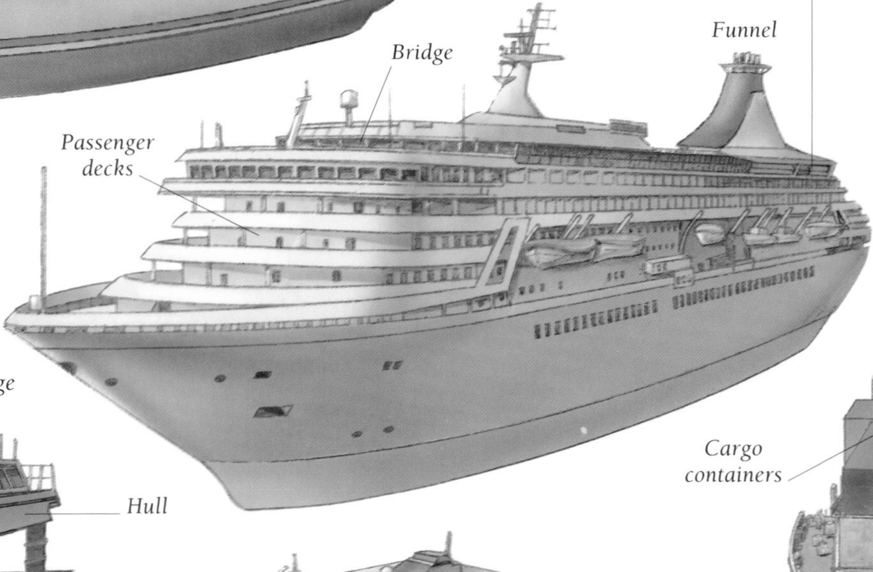

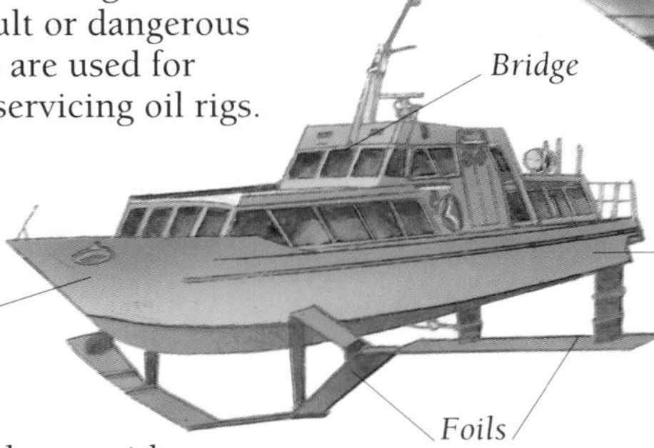

Bridge

Passenger decks

Bridge

Funnel

Cargo containers

Bridge

Hull

Bow (front)

Foils

Hydrofoil
Hydrofoils are boats with underwater "skis," called foils. As the boat gathers speed, the foils rise and lift the boat out of the water. The boat then skims across the surface of the water. Some hydrofoils can travel at speeds of more than 56 mph (90 km/h).

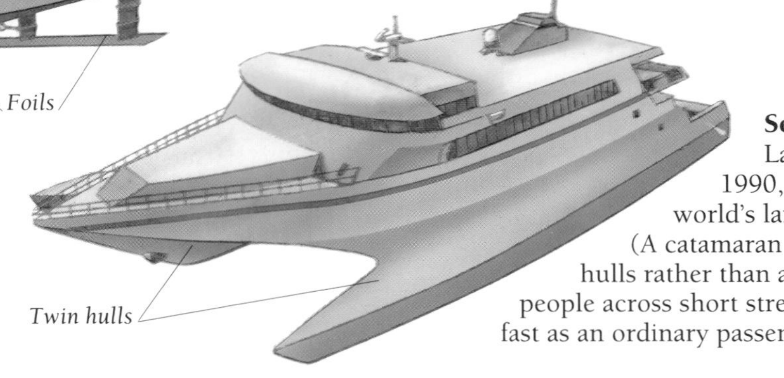

Twin hulls

Sea Cat
Launched in 1990, Sea Cat is the world's largest catamaran. (A catamaran is a boat with two hulls rather than a single hull.) It carries people across short stretches of water twice as fast as an ordinary passenger ferry.

Bow

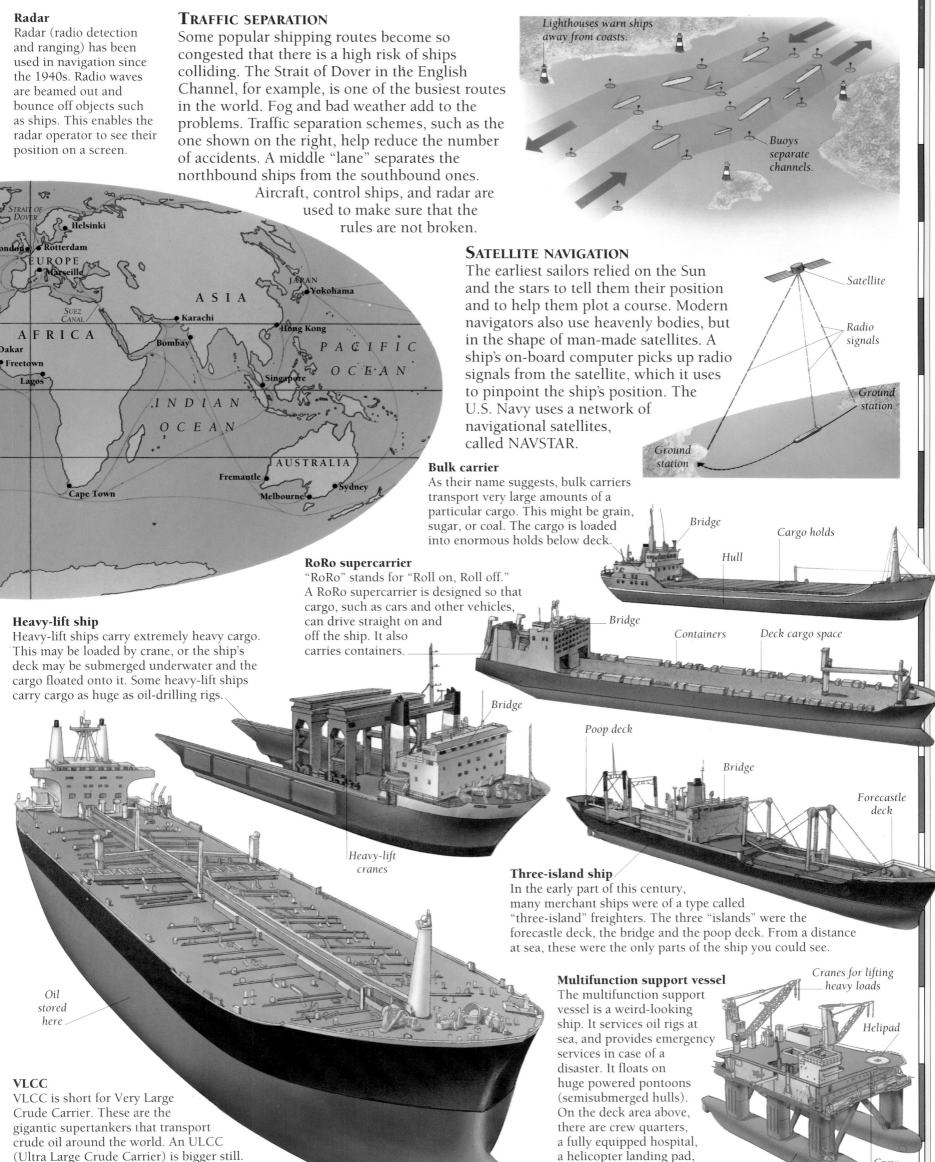

Radar

Radar (radio detection and ranging) has been used in navigation since the 1940s. Radio waves are beamed out and bounce off objects such as ships. This enables the radar operator to see their position on a screen.

TRAFFIC SEPARATION

Some popular shipping routes become so congested that there is a high risk of ships colliding. The Strait of Dover in the English Channel, for example, is one of the busiest routes in the world. Fog and bad weather add to the problems. Traffic separation schemes, such as the one shown on the right, help reduce the number of accidents. A middle "lane" separates the northbound ships from the southbound ones. Aircraft, control ships, and radar are used to make sure that the rules are not broken.

Lighthouses warn ships away from coasts.

Buoys separate channels.

SATELLITE NAVIGATION

The earliest sailors relied on the Sun and the stars to tell them their position and to help them plot a course. Modern navigators also use heavenly bodies, but in the shape of man-made satellites. A ship's on-board computer picks up radio signals from the satellite, which it uses to pinpoint the ship's position. The U.S. Navy uses a network of navigational satellites, called NAVSTAR.

Satellite

Radio signals

Ground station

Ground station

Bulk carrier

As their name suggests, bulk carriers transport very large amounts of a particular cargo. This might be grain, sugar, or coal. The cargo is loaded into enormous holds below deck.

Bridge

Hull

Cargo holds

RoRo supercarrier

"RoRo" stands for "Roll on, Roll off." A RoRo supercarrier is designed so that cargo, such as cars and other vehicles, can drive straight on and off the ship. It also carries containers.

Bridge

Containers

Deck cargo space

Heavy-lift ship

Heavy-lift ships carry extremely heavy cargo. This may be loaded by crane, or the ship's deck may be submerged underwater and the cargo floated onto it. Some heavy-lift ships carry cargo as huge as oil-drilling rigs.

Bridge

Heavy-lift cranes

Poop deck

Bridge

Forecastle deck

Three-island ship

In the early part of this century, many merchant ships were of a type called "three-island" freighters. The three "islands" were the forecastle deck, the bridge and the poop deck. From a distance at sea, these were the only parts of the ship you could see.

Multifunction support vessel

The multifunction support vessel is a weird-looking ship. It services oil rigs at sea, and provides emergency services in case of a disaster. It floats on huge powered pontoons (semisubmerged hulls). On the deck area above, there are crew quarters, a fully equipped hospital, a helicopter landing pad, and firefighting equipment.

Cranes for lifting heavy loads

Helipad

Crew quarters

Pontoon

Oil stored here

VLCC

VLCC is short for Very Large Crude Carrier. These are the gigantic supertankers that transport crude oil around the world. An ULCC (Ultra Large Crude Carrier) is bigger still. It can carry an amazing 492,000 tons (500,000 tonnes) of oil at a time.

Undersea Archaeology

UNDERSEA ARCHAEOLOGY involves the study of shipwrecks, sunken treasure, and even ruined cities which may have lain on the seabed for centuries. Before the invention of scuba gear in the 1940s, very little work could be done on deep-sea wrecks. Divers made a perilous descent in wooden diving bells. Despite this, some early salvage efforts were successful, retrieving mostly money and valuable objects such as silver, gold, and cannons.

Today, archaeologists have the latest diving technology and instruments to help them. By studying, mapping, and raising wrecks and artifacts, archaeologists have been able to discover valuable information about ships and shipboard life in the past. They have excavated coins, guns, clothes, shoes, and the remains of crew members themselves. Some of the most famous shipwrecks so far discovered include the *Titanic*, the *Wasa*, the Spanish treasure ships, and galleons that sailed with the Spanish Armada and which were wrecked off the west coast of Ireland.

This engraving from the 1600s shows an early salvage operation in progress.

MARINE ARCHAEOLOGISTS AT WORK

A marine archaeologist's job is much like that of an archaeologist on land. Once a site has been located, it must be surveyed and excavated before the artifacts can be raised to the surface and put on display. The large illustration shows some of the methods used by marine archaeologists. The work is painstaking – everything must be numbered, recorded, and studied. The marine archaeologist's task is made harder by the special problems of working underwater – the waves, currents, water pressure, low temperatures, and poor visibility.

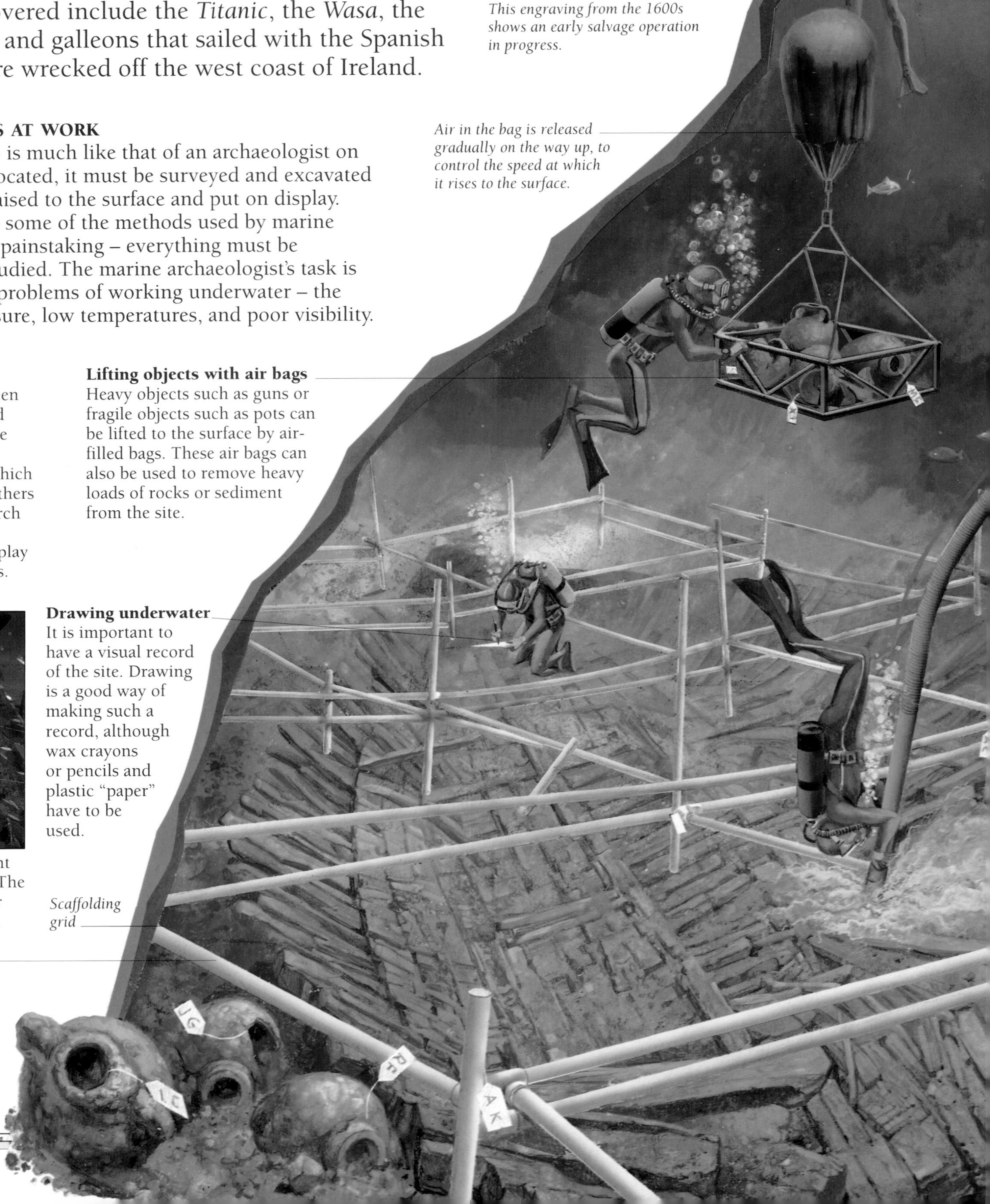

Air in the bag is released gradually on the way up, to control the speed at which it rises to the surface.

Locating a wreck site
Thousands of wreck sites have been discovered all over the world, and there are many more waiting to be found. Some are found simply by chance. They are often in areas which are popular with sports divers. Others may be found after years of research and reading. Modern underwater instruments, such as sonars, can play an important part in locating sites.

Lifting objects with air bags
Heavy objects such as guns or fragile objects such as pots can be lifted to the surface by air-filled bags. These air bags can also be used to remove heavy loads of rocks or sediment from the site.

Drawing underwater
It is important to have a visual record of the site. Drawing is a good way of making such a record, although wax crayons or pencils and plastic "paper" have to be used.

Archaeologists excavate an ancient wreck in the Mediterranean Sea. The cargo consisted of wine and other goods packed in amphorae (jars).

Scaffolding grid

Site mapping
Before a site can be excavated, it has to be surveyed and mapped in order to provide an accurate record of its contents. The site is divided into small squares, using a scaffolding or tape grid. Then each square is surveyed.

Raising the rafters
Large wooden timbers, such as these huge pieces from the stern of a wooden sailing ship, have to be winched to the surface so that they can be cleaned and preserved.

Preservation
Seawater preserves wood, leather, and other materials very well. But when they are brought to the surface, they need to be treated to stop them from drying out and crumbling. Various methods are used to preserve materials. Timbers are immersed in or sprayed with chemicals, such as polyethylene glycol (a type of wax). Iron may be roasted in a furnace with pure hydrogen to preserve it. Treatment can take years to complete.

UNDERWATER ARCHAEOLOGICAL SITES

There are two main types of archaeological sites to be found underwater. Wrecked ships and the artifacts they contain form one type. The other type are cities or harbors that have been drowned by changes in sea level or by natural disasters, such as tsunamis.

The *Batavia*
This archway was reconstructed from stones carried by the Dutch ship *Batavia*. It sank off the west coast of Australia in 1629. The wreck was found in 1961, but it was not excavated until 1972–76. Among other artifacts found were iron and bronze cannons, and silverware bound for India.

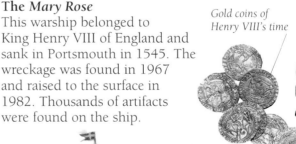

Roskilde Fjord
In 1959, divers found five different types of Viking ships in the waters of Roskilde Fjord, in Denmark. The ships had been deliberately filled with stones and sunk to block the fjord in about AD 1000. The wrecks were excavated by building a dam around them to keep the water away from the site.

The *Mary Rose*
This warship belonged to King Henry VIII of England and sank in Portsmouth in 1545. The wreckage was found in 1967 and raised to the surface in 1982. Thousands of artifacts were found on the ship.

Gold coins of Henry VIII's time

Blocks (pulleys) preserved in seawater for 437 years

Removing sediment
Many of the artifacts found on a site will be buried under layers of sand and mud called sediment. Some of this can simply be brushed or fanned off. Archaeologists also use pipelike devices called airlifts to remove sediment. These are like giant underwater vacuum cleaners powered by compressed air. Water-jets can also be used to wash sand and mud away.

Underwater photography
Besides drawing, photography is also used to keep an accurate record of a site. A fixed grid keeps the camera steady and helps to pinpoint the location of the photograph when it is developed. Series of photos are often linked together to form photomosaics. However, if the water is very murky, photography may not always be possible.

The Wasa as built in 1628

The *Wasa*
This was a Swedish warship that capsized and sank in Stockholm harbor on its first voyage in 1628. The *Wasa* was found by a marine archaeologist, Anders Franzen, in 1956. A huge rescue operation was launched to save the wreck, which was raised in one piece in 1961. It was gradually lifted off the seabed and into a dry dock, where it was sprayed with preservative.

The *Wasa* was raised on April 24, 1961. Here it finally breaks the surface, having been lifted by two floating cranes on either side. The *Wasa* and its artifacts are housed in a museum in Sweden.

Port Royal
In the seventeenth century, Port Royal was a wealthy pirate city near Kingston, Jamaica. In 1692, the city disappeared into the sea. It had been hit by an earthquake and tsunami. The city and 2,000 of its inhabitants were drowned. Most of the city only lay about 33 ft (10 m) below the surface, and some of its treasure was salvaged at once. But the city was not properly excavated until 1965–68. Three buildings were discovered still intact.

The Unhealthy Sea

FOR MANY YEARS, the sea has been used as the biggest dumping ground on Earth. The oceans are huge, but they cannot go on absorbing waste forever. Today, marine pollution is a serious problem in many parts of the world. Huge amounts of sewage, industrial waste, oil, plastics, and radioactive waste are dumped into the sea every year. Pollutants can kill or damage marine animals and plants, and destroy fragile ecosystems such as coral reefs. They may also be dangerous to people. Ocean pollution cannot be stopped completely, but efforts are being made to clean up the sea. Several international agreements are now in force. One of these, the Regional Seas Programme, was set up in 1975 to clean up the Mediterranean Sea, one of the most polluted stretches of seawater in the world.

Industrial waste

Many industries are based near the coast or along rivers. They often discharge chemical waste into the water. This includes heavy metals such as lead, mercury, cadmium, copper, and tin, which comes from mining, smelting, paper production, and so on. Metals such as lead and mercury can become concentrated and kill fish and animals higher up the food chain.

Factory waste pipes often empty directly into the sea and can endanger beaches.

Some heavy industries near coastlines pour out airborne pollution. The chemicals then fall into the sea.

SOURCES OF POLLUTION

There are two main sources of ocean pollution. More than 40 percent comes from the land. It is brought to the sea by rivers. Most of the rest is dumped or pumped directly into the sea. Pollution is also carried by the air. It falls into the sea with the rain.

Pesticides are sprayed by both tractor and airplane.

Pesticides pollute rivers and streams, which then flow into the sea.

Agricultural chemicals

With the growing demand for farmers to produce more food, more chemicals are sprayed on fields to kill pests and give bigger harvests. About half of these pesticides and fertilizers are washed off the fields by the rain and into the rivers. They are then carried to the sea. Some fertilizers reduce the amount of oxygen in the water, so animals cannot breathe. Pesticides, such as DDT, build up inside animals, poisoning them and the animals that eat them (see opposite page). DDT also causes seabirds to lay thin-shelled eggs that do not hatch.

Assorted garbage, nylon fishing nets, floats, and bottles foul beaches and coastlines around the world.

Some chemicals are emptied directly into the sea.

Garbage

Each year millions of tons of plastic rubbish, glass bottles, tins and metal drums, wood, old nets, and ropes are dumped in the sea. This "garbage" kills many seabirds and mammals that get entangled in it. Materials such as plastic take many years to decay. They are called nonbiodegradable.

Pesticides such as DDT can contaminate offshore shellfish beds.

Mussels

POLLUTION BLACK SPOTS

In seas that are almost surrounded by land, pollution can become very serious indeed. Here, pollutants do not get diluted as they do in the open ocean. The problem is made worse if the seas are in areas of heavy industry or shipping, or if a lot of people live near them. The worst affected areas are the Mediterranean, the North Sea, the Baltic Sea, and the Red Sea.

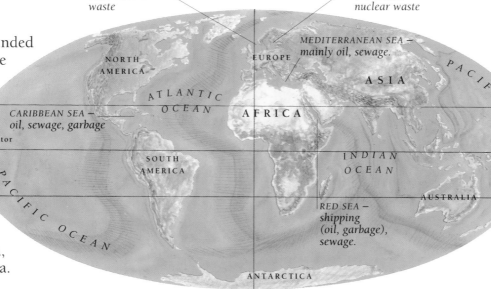

NORTH SEA — oil, industrial waste

BALTIC SEA — chemicals, nuclear waste

MEDITERRANEAN SEA — mainly oil, sewage.

CARIBBEAN SEA — oil, sewage, garbage

RED SEA — shipping (oil, garbage), sewage.

NORTH AMERICA

ATLANTIC OCEAN

EUROPE

ASIA

PACIFIC OCEAN

AFRICA

Equator

SOUTH AMERICA

INDIAN OCEAN

PACIFIC OCEAN

AUSTRALIA

ANTARCTICA

Oil spills

If an oil tanker crashes or runs aground, it can spill huge amounts of oil into the sea. It forms a slick that can be carried ashore by the wind and currents. Oil kills seabirds, whose feathers become clogged, and fish and mammals, who are poisoned by the oil they swallow. A spill has to be controlled quickly. Unfortunately, some of the detergents used to break the oil up are more dangerous to marine life than the oil itself.

Sewage dumping

In some places, untreated sewage is pumped straight into the sea. This can make the water unsafe for people to swim in because of the risk of infection. It can also rob the water of oxygen. Sewage contains nutrients that algae need. But too many nutrients can cause too rapid a growth. As they die, the algae use up extra oxygen from the water, and other creatures may suffocate. This process is called eutrophication (overfeeding).

Radioactive waste

Some parts of the deep sea have been used as dumping grounds for highly dangerous radio-active waste that has been encased in concrete. This can take thousands of years to break down and become safe. People are worried that it may leak into the water. In large quantities, it can kill fish and other creatures. In smaller amounts, it can cause cancers and abnormal growth.

When the tanker *Amoco Cadiz* ran aground and burned off the coast of France in 1978, the oil pollution was the worst the world had seen up to that date.

If the oil catches fire, thick smoke billows into the sky, polluting the air as well.

Poisonous waste from the smoke falls into the sea.

A ruptured oil tanker spills huge amounts of oil per hour into the sea.

Booms are placed around the oil to try to stop it from spreading.

Sewage being dumped at sea.

Incinerator ships

These burn toxic waste at sea. However, the burning itself gives off poisonous waste. They are now banned in many places.

Boat dumping radioactive waste barrels.

FATAL FOOD CHAIN

Some pollutants have devastating effects if they enter the food chain. They build up in animals' bodies, becoming more concentrated as they pass up the chain. Two of the worst offenders are the pesticide DDT and the metal mercury. Fish that have eaten DDT-contaminated food may contain 35 times as much DDT as the food they have eaten. The dose becomes even stronger in the next link of the chain, which is a larger fish or even a person. In 1952, a chemical factory in Japan leaked mercury into the sea. More than 100 people died and more than 2,000 were paralyzed by eating fish and shellfish poisoned by the mercury.

Animals cannot excrete the DDT in their bodies. Instead, it builds up in their tissues.

Squat lobster

Plaice eat small crustaceans and mollusks.

Plaice

Mackerel eat small crustaceans and fish. At each step of the food chain, the DDT poison builds up, so that the feeder at the next step up receives a larger dose.

Mackerel

Humans eating contaminated fish receive the biggest DDT dose of all.

Cod eat smaller fish. By this stage the poison has become highly concentrated.

Cod

Future Use of the Oceans

WE ALREADY EXPLOIT MANY of the resources found in the world's oceans. These include both renewable resources that can be replaced, and nonrenewable resources that are used once, then lost. Fish, for example, have been a rich source of food for thousands of years. But only if stocks are properly managed and overfishing is prevented, will there be enough fish in the future. Nonrenewable ocean resources include minerals, oil, and natural gas. World oil and gas supplies are limited, but the oceans have vast, untapped energy resources. In the future, electricity derived from tidal or wave energy, or from the heat energy stored in seawater, may replace power from oil, gas, or coal. To safeguard the future use of the oceans, however, we must safeguard the future of the oceans themselves. Land-based pollution, such as sewage and chemicals, spilled oil, and waste dumped by ships are in danger of turning the oceans into a huge garbage dump. The future depends on keeping the oceans healthy and clean.

NONRENEWABLE RESOURCES

Nonrenewable resources cannot be replaced once they are used, at least not for millions of years. In the oceans, this means minerals such as oil and manganese. There are also metal-rich muds, found around ocean ridges, which contain zinc, silver, and copper; aggregates (sand and gravel); and deposits of tin, gold, and even diamonds. Oil is already exploited, and other minerals may become as important.

Fossil fuels

Approximately 20 percent of the world's oil supply comes from beneath the seabed. At present most fossil fuels – oil, coal, and natural gas – are taken from the relatively shallow waters near the shore. Today, stocks are running low and may have run out altogether in 50 years' time. To meet the continuing demand, fossil fuel reserves in deeper waters will no doubt be exploited.

Manganese nodules

Billions of tons (tonnes) of manganese nodules – small, potato-shaped lumps rich in valuable metals – are found on the seafloor. Manganese nodules were first discovered in the 1870s. But it was not until the 1950s that scientists became interested in mining them commercially. Several methods of gathering the nodules and bringing them to the surface have been tested, including a suction device similar to a huge undersea vacuum cleaner.

KEY TO MAIN MAP
∴∵ EXTENSIVE MANGANESE NODULES
⧄ METAL-RICH SEDIMENTS
• SALT EXTRACTED FROM SEAWATER
▢ SEAWATER SUITABLE TEMPERATURE FOR OTEC SITE
◆ POTENTIAL OTEC SITE
◇ OPERATIONAL OTEC SITE
■ POTENTIAL TIDAL POWER SITE
□ OPERATIONAL TIDAL POWER SITE
🦐 FARMING OF CRUSTACEANS
🦪 FARMING OF OYSTERS
CONCENTRATION OF KRILL
🌿 SEAWEED HARVESTING

GREENLAND

Frobisher Bay

Cook Inlet

Strait of Georgia

NORTH AMERICA

Bay of Fundy

ATLANTIC OCEAN

Rio Colorado

Miami
BAHAMAS
Baja California
CUBA
PUERTO RICO
HAWAII
ST. CROIX

PACIFIC OCEAN

São Luis

SOUTH AMERICA

Golfo Nuevo
Golfo de San Jorge
Santa Cruz
Strait of Magellan

ANTARCTICA

Salt is raked into piles at these sea salt pans near Goa, India (right).

Extracting salt from the sea

About 5.9 million tons (6 million tonnes) of salt are extracted from the sea every year. In hot countries, such as those in Asia and around the Mediterranean, seawater is channelled into large, shallow pans along the coast. The Sun's heat evaporates the water, leaving the salt behind. In some desert countries near the Persian Gulf, coastal desalination plants extract the salt from seawater to produce fresh drinking-water supplies.

Krill fishing

Someday you might eat the same meal as a whale – Antarctic krill. Scientists are studying ways of using krill as a food source for humans. Of the 4,900 million tons (5,000 million tonnes) of krill in the sea around Antarctica, up to 98.5 million tons (100 million tonnes) could be harvested each year. Some krill is already caught in nets, like the one shown on the left, and frozen or made into paste.

ENERGY RESOURCES

As supplies of fossil fuels run out, and as concern grows about the harm such fuels are doing to the environment, scientists are looking for alternative sources of energy. Energy from the Sun is stored in the Earth's atmosphere and oceans. This solar energy powers the winds, waves, and currents, all potentially clean and renewable sources of energy. About three-quarters of solar energy reaching the Earth is absorbed by the oceans. The heat energy of the water itself could also be used. A system called OTEC (Ocean Thermal Energy Conversion) uses the temperature difference between warm surface water and colder deep water to generate electricity. The map below shows the places where the OTEC system is already in operation, or where it could be used in the future.

La Rance tidal power station (above) in Brittany, France, lies across an estuary that empties into the Atlantic Ocean. The station opened in 1967.

Tidal energy

The tidal power station built across the mouth of the Rance River in France uses the energy of the tides to generate electricity. It consists of a dam with 24 tunnels running through it. Each contains a generator. As the tides rise and fall, the water rushes up and down the tunnels, turning the generators to produce electricity. Two other sites with great tidal energy potential are the Bay of Fundy, Canada, and the estuary of the Severn River, England.

BIOLOGICAL RESOURCES

The oceans' biological resources include natural fisheries and fish farming (or mariculture). Fish farming is big business in many parts of the world. Several species, such as tiger prawns and salmon, are now farmed intensively. Scientists are looking for new, unlikely food sources that could be exploited in the future, such as seaweed, krill, and deep-sea fishes.

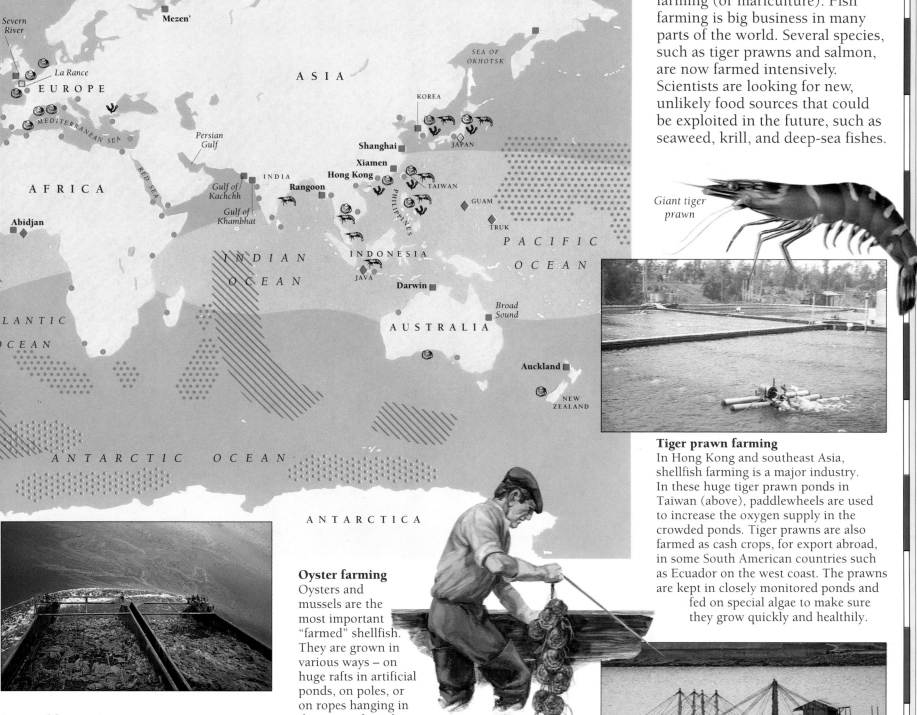

Giant tiger prawn

Tiger prawn farming

In Hong Kong and southeast Asia, shellfish farming is a major industry. In these huge tiger prawn ponds in Taiwan (above), paddlewheels are used to increase the oxygen supply in the crowded ponds. Tiger prawns are also farmed as cash crops, for export abroad, in some South American countries such as Ecuador on the west coast. The prawns are kept in closely monitored ponds and fed on special algae to make sure they grow quickly and healthily.

Oyster farming

Oysters and mussels are the most important "farmed" shellfish. They are grown in various ways – on huge rafts in artificial ponds, on poles, or on ropes hanging in the sea, such as those on the Spanish oyster boat on the right. This makes them simpler to harvest. The oysters are not given special food; they get their nourishment from the sea, just as they would in the wild. They are simply thinned out as they grow and protected from predators.

Seaweed harvesting

Like krill, seaweed may become an important food source in the future. It is rich in vitamins and minerals, and grows abundantly in many areas, although it can be difficult to collect. The photo above shows kelp being harvested off the coast of California. In China and Japan, several types of seaweed are specially cultivated for food.

Index

ACKNOWLEDGMENTS

Dorling Kindersley would like to thank Martyn Foote, Christopher Gillingwater, Roger Bullen and DK Cartography, Anna Kunst, Lynn Bresler, and Peter Hunter. 3-D representations of the seafloor supplied by the Institute of Oceanographic Sciences Deacon Laboratory from data provided by the British Oceanographic Data Centre, NERC, on behalf of the OOC/IHO General Bathymetric Chart of the Oceans (GEBCO). Permission to use Map of World Ocean Floor by Bruce C. Heezen and Marie Tharp, 1977 (© Marie Tharp 1977) as reference kindly granted by Marie Tharp, 1 Washington Ave, South Nyack, NY 10960.

Additional illustrations Richard Ward, Jon Rogers, Andrea Corbella, and Fiona Bell Currie
Picture research Sarah Moule

Picture Credits
t=top, b=bottom, l=left, r=right, c=center, a=above

Ardea Ltd., London/A. Warren: 55bc; Bruce Coleman Ltd.: 35cr; /G. Cubitt: 62clb; /I. Everson: 62br; /J. Foott: 63bl; /J. Stein Grove: 25tr; /B. Wood: 30bl; /C. Zuber: 52ca; © Photothèque Electricité de France: 63tr; Mary Evans Picture Library: 10tr, 14cra; Robert Harding Picture Library/Bildagentur Schuster/Scholz: 41c; /A. Tovy: 31tr; /A. Woolfitt/Readers Digest: 59cr; The Image Bank/L. Fried: 53tl; /D. King: 43br; /J. Schmitt: 33tr; Institute of Oceanographic Sciences/B. Bett: 16c, 17bl; Frank Lane Picture Agency: 23cr; /H. Hollinger: 45tr; /D.P. Wilson: 51tc, 51tr; /D.P. Wilson/E. & A. Hosking: 12tr; NHPA/B. Hawkes: 8bl; /S. Krasemann: 39ca; /D. Woodfall: 60cl; Netherlands Board of Tourism: 49br; Oxford Scientific Films Ltd./M. Gibbs: 35cla; /H. Hall: 13tr; Planet Earth Pictures/R. Hessler: 21bl, 26r, 28b, 36bl;

/Joyce Photographics: 40c; J. Lythgoe: 14tc, 21bc, 63br; /D. Perrine: 4t; /C. Petron: 58bl; /P. Scoones: 35clb; /F. Schulke: 11cb; /N. Wu: 19tl; Rex Features Ltd./Sipa Press: 61tl; /Sipa Press/L.Chamussy: 49crb; Tim Ridley: 61br; Ann Ronan at Image Select: 58tr; By permission of The Royal College of Surgeons of England/Courtesy of Mr. G.P. Darwin: 21br; Science Photo Library/S. Fraser: 8br, 39ca, 60t; /NASA: 45tl, 47tr; /D. Parker: 37br; South American Pictures/T. Morrison: 17cr; Sygma/Giraud: 44bc; Telegraph Colour Library/Colorific/Black Star/K. Sakamoto: 23t; Tropix/J. Wickins: 63cr; Courtesy of the Vasa Museum, Stockholm: 59bc; Viewfinder: 54cra; Vikingeskibshallen i Roskilde: 59t; Tony Waltham Geophotos: 48tc; Woods Hole Oceanographic Institution: 15cr.

Every effort has been made to trace the copyright holders and we apologize for any unintentional omissions. We would be pleased to insert the appropriate acknowledgment in any subsequent edition of this publication.